To :. MOTHER
in Mother's Day
2002

With ♡
BRIAN & HAPPY

pots &
containers

ANTHONY ATHA

pots &
containers

MARKS &
SPENCER

Marks and Spencer p.l.c.

Baker Street, London W1U 8EP

www.marksandspencer.com

Created and produced by The Bridgewater Book Company Ltd.

ISBN: 1-84273-533-0

Printed in China

NOTE

For growing and harvesting, calendar information applies
only to the Northern Hemisphere (US zones 5–9).

contents

introduction   **6**

containers for gardens   **8**
   window boxes   *10*
   hanging baskets   *12*
   containers for large plants   *14*
   smaller containers   *16*

using containers in gardens   **18**
   the importance of planning   *20*
   containers as focal points   *22*
   creating rooms and features   *24*
   containers in doors and arches   *26*
   containers on steps and paths   *28*

colour schemes in containers   **30**
   creating a colour scheme   *32*
   hot planting schemes   *34*
   cool planting schemes   *38*
   blue and white schemes   *40*
   pale pink and red schemes   *42*

seasonal ideas   **44**
   container gardening in winter   *46*
   container gardening in spring   *50*
   container gardening in summer   *54*
   container gardening in autumn   *58*

plant directory   **62**
   trees   *64*
   conifers   *66*
   shrubs   *67*
   small roses   *69*
   climbing roses   *70*
   climbers and wall plants   *72*
   perennials   *74*
   annuals and bedding plants   *79*
   spring bulbs   *88*
   summer and autumn-flowering bulbs   *90*

index   **94**

introduction

Growing plants in attractive containers has increased in popularity during recent years and especially with gardeners who have small gardens; it is an ideal way to decorate walls, windows and patios with plants that reveal colourful flowers and leaves. Additionally, it is a practical way to grow plants at the entrances to town houses and at the sides of cottage doors. Few eyes are not captivated by a pair of neatly-clipped, half-standard Sweet Bay trees in Versailles-type planters and positioned on either side of a door, and especially one that is surrounded by a white wall. The Sweet Bay, also known as Bay Laurel, is evergreen and its glossy, mid- to dark green leaves create a distinctive and stately feature throughout the year. It has the bonus of the leaves being used in cooking. This all-colour book is both inspirational and practical and seeks to guide both novice and experienced gardeners through the ways to use plants in containers, to improve patios, courtyards, raised decks and roof gardens, as well as their use throughout a garden, perhaps at the sides of paths and steps and as focal points. The range of containers is wide and some, such as windowboxes, have seasonal displays which can be changed two or three times a year, while large tubs provide permanent homes for small trees and shrubs. Traditional clay pots can be used for seasonal plants, from stately lilies at ground level to small pots placed in plant holders secured to walls and fences. Fruit, vegetables and herbs can be grown in containers, but it is essential to choose fruit trees which are growing on a dwarfing rootstock and vegetables and herbs that suit the container. Tomatoes, for example, can be grown in both large pots and growing-bags on warm, sunny patios, while potatoes are certain candidates for proprietary potato-planting containers that provide a wealth of soil. Alternatively – and perhaps more innovatively – potatoes can be grown in a stack of three or four small car tyres wired together. The tyres can be made more pleasing to the eye by painting them white.

Creating seasonal displays

The practicalities and philosophy of ensuring seasonal displays is thoroughly described in this practical book, with advice on reliable plants and varieties for winter, spring, summer and autumn features. Bulbs are mainly used for spring displays, with half-hardy bedding plants creating the majority of colour in summer displays in hanging baskets and window boxes. Autumn and winter displays can be rich in coloured foliage provided by small, evergreen shrubs and miniature conifers, as well as from berried shrubs. Variegated small-leaved ivies are ideal for autumn and winter displays and with their trailing stems help to create a relaxed display as well as to unify one plant with another.

What plants to use?

Choosing the right plants for containers is an essential part of successful container gardening and towards the back of this book there is a comprehensive parade of them – many illustrated. They include bulbs, herbaceous perennials, annuals and biennials, shrubs, trees and climbers. Each plant is described, with information about size and shape, so that it will not be too large or too small for its chosen position. Incidentally, many shrubs and trees may eventually have to be removed to the garden when they out-size the container or position. A further facet of this chapter is lists of plants to suit specific positions in gardens, from full sun to shade. Soil and compost preferences are also featured. Additionally, if you desire fragrantly flowered plants for your containers there are detailed lists to help you choose, as well as plants that create an alpine garden, perhaps in stone sinks on a patio or terrace.

containers
for gardens

Window boxes rich in colour throughout the year create distinctive features under windows, while hanging baskets are superb for brightening walls, porches and balconies. And for a dramatic display position hanging baskets on either side of a window, with a richly coloured window box beneath. Large containers such as Versailles planters, tubs and Ali Baba jars create dramatic homes for plants, while small plants in terracotta pots can be put in brackets secured to walls and fences.

window boxes

Attractive window boxes can be marvels of ingenuity, both in design and colour. Successful window box gardening takes thought, time and care. Each one is rather like a semi-permanent flower arrangement and many of the rules that apply to flower arranging also apply to window box gardening.

Practical aspects

There are a number of practical things to consider. First, the window box must fit on or beneath a window and it must be securely fastened in place. It will be fairly heavy when full of plants and compost, and anyone planning a window box overhanging a street must be certain that it is retained securely in position. This is usually done by securing metal brackets to the wall. (If you are not an expert get

▲ *This window box includes variegated ivy, small tobacco plants, verbena, helichrysum and pansies in a carefully controlled design.*

professional help.) In this type of position make certain that the window box has safety chains which can be secured to the wall or the window frame.

Window boxes must also blend in with the building. Normally they are made of wood or plastic, and can be painted to match the colour of the paintwork around the window. They must also be able to drain freely. The bottom must have a number of drainage holes and if it is placed flat on a windowsill, it should be supported on and raised by wood battens to facilitate good drainage. If this is not done then the plants will suffer as they become waterlogged, and the base of the window box will rot if it is made of wood.

Window boxes, indeed all containers, need watering frequently and they need feeding at least once a fortnight. They do not contain a large amount of compost, and therefore the plants will need additional encouragement if they are to grow properly. This is particularly true when you are growing vegetables and fruit.

MAKING A WINDOW BOX

If you cannot buy a window box that will fit your windowsill, the solution is to build your own. This is not difficult as long as you have some basic carpentry skills and the right tools. The most important thing is to measure the window space and wood accurately. There is nothing more aggravating than finding the window box is a bit too long, and it is quite easy to do this if you forget to add the thickness of the wood on both sides.

Secure the sides and the bottom firmly using battens to hold them in place. Use good screws and do not just nail one piece of wood to another. Treat all the timber with wood preservative before you start (using proper preservative that will not damage the plants) and drill drainage holes in the bottom. Then, when the box is complete, line it with polythene, holding this in place with staples (use a staple gun). Finally, cut out matching holes in the liner to marry up with the drainage holes, and the box is ready for planting. A window box treated in this way should give good service for many years.

▶ *Careful planning has created this brilliant yellow window box using broom (genista), ivy and chrysanthemums.*

assembling the window box

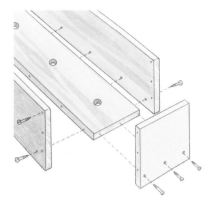

1 Measure the space and cut all the timber to size. Drill holes for the screws or, preferably, use battens to hold the sides and bottom in place.

2 When you have screwed the window box firmly together, line it with heavy-duty polythene to prevent the timber rotting. Staple the lining in place.

3 If the window box is freestanding fix it to the wall with brackets as shown. Make sure these are really secure and attach safety chains to the sides.

hanging baskets

Hanging baskets are one of the glories of summer and brighten porches, city streets and balconies. They are not all that difficult to manage and maintain, but you do have to take care when choosing the plants if you want to achieve the best effect.

A blue, red and white basket

For a 40cm/16in diameter hanging basket you will need: six trailing plants such as…

Glechoma hederacea 'Variegata' – trailing ground ivy, blue-green leaves with white edges, sometimes has lilac flowers in the summer.

Hedera helix (ivy) – use small-leaved variegated varieties such as 'Adam', 'Glacier' or 'Eva'.

Plectranthus forsteri 'Marginatus' – trailing, variegated green and white leaves.

Sutera cordata – small bright green leaves;

▶ *This is another red, white and blue design using ageratum and begonias for a blue and red effect. Start planting at the base of the basket and push the plants through the wire from inside to the outside. Keep the plant as intact as possible.*

❶ Begonia (red)
❷ Ageratum (blue)
❸ Petunia (white)
❹ Lobelia (blue)
❺ Ivy

the variety 'Snowflake' has small white flowers in summer.

Also use…

3–6 trailing *Pelargonium* 'Breakaway Red'.

1–2 *Pelargonium* 'Sensation Scarlet' for the top of the basket, or red dwarf plants from the 'Video Mixed' series.

6–9 *Petunia* 'Falcon White'.

6 *Lobelia* 'Sapphire' – violet blue with a white eye or 'Kathleen Mallard' – blue.

Larger or smaller baskets may require more or fewer plants, bearing in mind that it is best to overcrowd the basket for

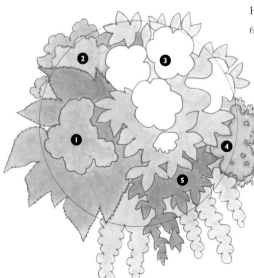

maximum effect. Plant the trailing foliage plants around the rim of the basket to trail down the sides, and plant the coloured plants in bands. They will grow through the trailing green-leaved ivy, *Hedera*, and make an increasing impact throughout the summer.

A yellow and orange hanging basket for maximum impact

For a 40cm/16in diameter hanging basket you will need…

6–9 trailing *Tropaeolum majus* (nasturtium), either Double Gleam Hybrids or Alaska Mixed.

6 *Lysimachia congestiflora* (loosestrife) – clumps of yellow tubular flowers with red centres.

6 *Bidens ferulifolia* – small yellow star-shaped flowers that cascade down the sides of the basket.

6 *Tagetes* (marigold) – 'Honeycomb' is reddish-orange with yellow-edged flowers; 'Red Marietta' has brilliant red-orange single flowers with fine yellow edges; and 'Orange Boy', deep orange.

▲ *Hanging baskets can be used as part of the overall garden design. The main plants used in this fragrant garden are scented geraniums.*

▶ *Deep pink and white busy Lizzies make a simple two-coloured basket. Other similar baskets echo the planting in the garden.*

A hanging basket for the winter months

Almost all hanging baskets are planted for summer display, but you can contrive an attractive mixture of plants that will give colour throughout the winter provided you can keep the basket in a relatively frost-free environment. The basis for a winter basket is hardy evergreen plants that provide a green backdrop. The plants to include are…
Hedera helix 'Glacier' or *H. h.* 'Pin Oak' (both ivies) – if the basket is in an exposed position make sure you choose varieties that are fully hardy.
Polypodium vulgare – an evergreen fern.

Vinca minor (lesser periwinkle) – evergreen, with trailing shoots and flowers from early in spring to autumn.
Viola x wittrockiana (pansy) – either choose mixed colours or plain blue or white varieties. They provide colour for months over the winter.

Simple baskets for summer colour

Some of the most effective hanging baskets are those where only one plant is used, often in a variety of colours. The best annual for a tonal basket is the petunia. There are three types: grandiflora, the one with the largest flowers up to 12.5cm/5in across;

multiflora, with each plant carrying many flowers, single or double up to 7.5cm/3in across; and milliflora, smaller plants carrying many flowers. Most petunias are in shades of red, pink, purple and white. Plants from the Celebrity Mixed Series, the Celebrity Bunting Series (darker colours), and Celebrity Pastel Mixed Series, produce matching displays with a random variety of colour. Single colour petunias, such as 'Chiffon Morn' in pink and Supercascade White are also good. The grandiflora petunias include Aladdin Mixed in some startling colours, including deep purple, and Banana Milkshake in yellow and white.

containers for large plants

It stands to reason that large plants need large containers, especially if they are going to grow successfully. Much thought should be given to purchasing larger containers, as they are often expensive, and it is important that they fit into the style that you have decided on for your garden.

Containers for large plants

If you want to grow large plants, you have got to think big. In fact all large plants, trees, fruit and shrubs will need as large a container as you can provide if they are to flourish and attain anything like their potential proportions. They are best grown in raised beds or in special large containers to match the overall design of the patio, roof garden or terrace. All containers need good drainage at the bottom, and an automatic watering system is of great assistance.

The next key factor is style – you have to think carefully about how a large expensive container will fit into the garden, and how the container will relate to the type and style of the plant. Trees or shrubs with a spreading habit look best in wide-brimmed pots, and formal clipped topiarised trees need formal containers to look their best. Very often large containers are made from terracotta, but other materials, such as stone or glazed earthenware, are also suitable provided they can accommodate the root system of the plant. Also, keep

◀ *Canna lilies contribute to a garden planned to give the feeling of a tropical forest. Heat and sun are necessary for success.*

the containers and their contents in proportion. It is always possible to pot on a tree into a larger container as it grows, while a small plant alone in a large pot will look bare and isolated. It is best to fill the space around the main plant with low-growing herbs or annuals to keep the planting in proportion.

Half-barrels

Half-barrels make good containers and can accommodate quite large trees. They look natural and suit almost any surrounding. You may be able to find old barrels in a junk shop, scrap yard, or even at your local brewery available at a discount. If you are lucky enough to get some barrels they need to be cut in half. Do this carefully with a saw, marking the circumference with a chalk line to guide you. Then fill the barrel with water and leave it overnight so that the wood swells. You may have to soak the barrel for even longer if the wood has become extremely dry. Then make drainage holes in the bottom and line the barrel with a thick plastic liner, holding it in place with staples. Make holes in the liner at the bottom to fit the drainage holes. Trim the plastic neatly before filling the barrel with hardcore and compost.

Positioning tall pots to the best advantage

Tall pots make excellent features on a patio garden and hardly need any plants to make them attractive. Ali Baba pots, in particular, are very decorative on their own but be careful if you are planning to plant up a very tall pot. There are few plants that work well and you should aim for some trailing nasturtium, *Tropaeolum*, or something equally simple.

Very large containers need to be placed carefully in the garden, and care has to be taken over the colour of the pot and the background that it is against. The design of a garden is composed of many things and background colour and planting are often overlooked.

The shape of the container often dictates the type of plant. Trees suit Versailles tubs while trailing nasturtiums fit Ali Baba jars.

DRAINAGE FEET

Although it does not matter in every case it can be very important to keep the base of the container off the ground. This particularly applies to window boxes and any container made from wood or MDF. Raise them using wooden battens or tiles. Special feet are available for most terracotta pots and they should be placed underneath to let the water drain away freely. Half-barrels should always be placed on bricks.

▶ *Foliage plants look good in spectacular containers. Here the blue-grey leaves of the agave tone in with the colour of the jars, and the spiky leaves contrast well.*

smaller containers

The smaller the space the more care has to be taken to choose containers that fit the garden design and match the plants. Often the small containers in a grouping get ignored; take care to see they blend with the others. Wall pots, too, are most important and can extend the garden upwards.

Small containers for small spaces

When it comes to choosing small containers there is a considerable choice, and with a little imagination the gardener can achieve great effects in a tiny space. Often in small gardens there is only room for a few plants, and each can be matched individually to the container. Small pots can be grouped together with small plants, such as primroses, *Primula* spp. or violas, while larger flat-bottomed bowls can be filled with rosette-shaped *Sempervivum*s that rejoice in the common name of house leek.

The important point is to focus on your favourite plants – small lavender bushes, spring bulbs, herbs and colourful annuals. Then collect a number of similar terracotta pots in varying sizes, plant them up and arrange them to suit the space. There may even be room for one or two climbing plants, such as a clematis, that can be trained up the wall of the house if a larger pot can be found to accommodate their root systems. Clematis like their roots to be cool, so shade the pots of clematis from the sun if

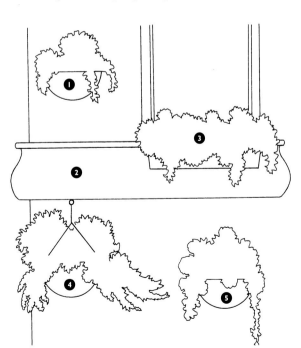

◀ *When the gardener is restricted to a small space such as a balcony then there is often scope to add hanging baskets and window boxes to extend the number of plants that can be grown. Make sure that these plantings match each other in style or the effect may be incongruous.*

❶ Wall pot
❷ Balcony outside window
❸ Window box
❹ Hanging basket
❺ Wall pot

ANTIQUE WALL POTS

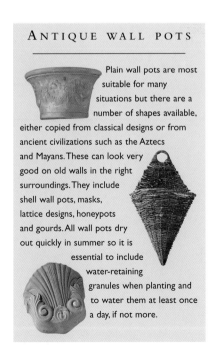

Plain wall pots are most suitable for many situations but there are a number of shapes available, either copied from classical designs or from ancient civilizations such as the Aztecs and Mayans. These can look very good on old walls in the right surroundings. They include shell wall pots, masks, lattice designs, honeypots and gourds. All wall pots dry out quickly in summer so it is essential to include water-retaining granules when planting and to water them at least once a day, if not more.

▶ *Ordinary terracotta pots secured to a garden fence with wire rings, planted with bright busy Lizzies to make everyone sit up and notice.*

you can. Even if you do not have a lot of room many lovely effects can be created with a bit of imagination.

Wall pots and hanging baskets

Container-only gardeners should always be aware of the vertical dimension. There is enormous scope to extend a garden upwards, given a suitable wall, or even some firm trellis, using a variety of wall pots. These are half-pots with flat backs that fit against a wall and hold plants that trail over the edge. If you fill these half-pots with colourful annuals they make a series of colour splashes. Used with imagination, the keen gardener can paint a series of abstract pictures using the flowers and plants.

There are many kinds of wall pots, including honeypots, decorated and plain shells, and fluted and rounded terracotta, emulating the styles of full pots. If you have a number of terracotta pots in the garden of varying shapes and designs, try to match the half-pots to the full ones, integrating the design. Also make sure that they are firmly secured to the wall, and that you can reach them easily with a hose extension for watering. Being that much more in the sun they will require watering as frequently as hanging baskets. Finally, when planting wall pots ensure, as far as possible, that the plants will flower at the same time. That way you will obtain the maximum effect.

Hanging baskets

Most hanging baskets are plain, made from wire, and the two most common sizes are 40cm/16in and 30cm/12in diameter. You can buy ornate filigree metal baskets if you want but the plain ones are generally better as the metalwork is soon obscured by the plants. Make sure that the hook and beam on which the basket hangs is strong and secure. Hanging baskets weigh a surprising amount when they are in full growth and have been watered. Ensure they can be reached for watering.

Both wall pots and hanging baskets are especially useful for balconies. Unless the balcony is very large, it is unlikely that there will be room enough for large containers or a raised bed big enough to accommodate climbers. In this situation, carefully positioned wall pots and hanging baskets provide colour and interest.

using containers
in gardens

The careful selection and positioning of containers is important and will further enhance your garden. Containers can be used in several ways, such as creating focal points within gardens and on patios, forming areas of seclusion and privacy and enhancing steps and paths. And choosing containers and plants that harmonize with each other, as well as with their backgrounds, is fundamental to getting the best from plants in containers, whether on a patio or in a garden area.

the importance of planning

The first thing you have to do when planning a garden is to measure the available space accurately. This is particularly important when planning a small patio garden, because the smaller the space, the more care is needed to ensure that every part of the garden is used to the very best advantage.

What is the garden used for?

Once you have measured and assessed the garden, you need to think how it can be used by the family. Space is the key. In a very small garden there may only be room for a table and chairs, somewhere to eat outside in summer. In such a restricted space the gardener may have to be content with just a few containers filled with herbs for the kitchen, or summer annuals and flowering climbers to brighten up the walls.

The larger the garden though, the more possibilities there are and the more problems that might occur. First, think

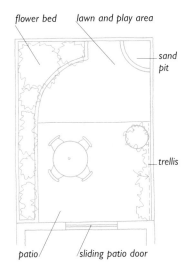

flower bed   lawn and play area

sand pit

trellis

patio   sliding patio door

▲ *A small garden at the rear of a town house. The trellis and tree on the right help to break up the space.*

◀ *A well-designed patio with a splendid hosta in a container. The bright orange and yellow flowers of the nasturtiums complement the green foliage.*

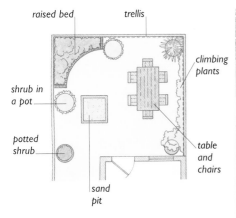

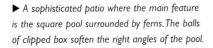

raised bed   trellis

climbing plants

shrub in a pot

potted shrub

table and chairs

sand pit

▲ *A smaller version of the design on page 20 for a town house with a side passage. The sand pit can be seen from the kitchen. The containers provide accent points around the edges.*

▶ *A sophisticated patio where the main feature is the square pool surrounded by ferns. The balls of clipped box soften the right angles of the pool.*

about the family. Many boys fancy themselves as young football stars but ball games and plants do not mix, and hydrangeas do not make good goal posts. Girls are usually quieter, but all children are likely to want an area to ride their tricycles and very young children appreciate a small sand pit, which can often be included even in a small patio garden. (If you include one make sure it can be covered against the unwelcome attentions of neighbouring cats.)

The vital questions It is a good idea to draw up a series of questions. Is the garden for eating outside in the summer? Is it an extra room? Does the family sit there? How much competition for the space is there between the gardening and

non-gardening members of the family? When you have answered these questions you can answer some of the specific gardening queries. Which direction does the garden face? How much sun does it get, or is it totally shaded? Once these questions have been answered you can decide, for example, whether there is room for a raised bed around a patio area, the type of containers that you need to purchase, and the type of plants that you want to grow. Raised beds have many advantages – they are more easily reached by the elderly and disabled, they provide sufficient space for more permanent trees and shrubs, and they give a container garden more substance. If you are planning to build a raised bed, do allow space between it and the walls

of the house, otherwise the damp course will get blocked and become damaged.

Essential rules Whether the space is large or small, certain rules apply. All the elements of a container garden must be easily reachable, and there must be a clear plan to the area. This may seem obvious and unnecessary but it guarantees essential factors, such as space to walk out of the back door. It also ensures that you can reach all the containers to water them properly, and that you can reach permanent plants to train or prune them as necessary. Don't forget you will need easy access to any outside tap for watering purposes, and make sure that kitchen windows will not end up covered with foliage that blocks out the light.

containers as focal points

Nothing is more challenging to the garden designer than an ordinary narrow rectangular garden, open to view, revealing everything. This is not what gardening should be. All gardens, even the smallest, need secrets, and the judicial use of containers can help the designer add many little extras.

A small formal garden using containers

Formal gardens are laid out in geometric patterns and have developed from the Elizabethan knot gardens of the late 16th century. Squares, rectangles and circles are the easiest shapes to use, and they can look very good in a small space. Faced with a fairly narrow rectangle the garden designer could start by narrowing the shape even further. Plant a dark green yew hedge around the garden or, if there is not room, train dark ivy up all the walls. Then, build a brick or flagged path right down the centre of the garden leading to a striking container at the end to draw the eye down the path, through the garden. Next, divide the garden more or less into four equal parts by creating a circle in the centre. This gives you four equal borders with a quadrant cut out of each in the centre. Edge each quadrant with box, *Buxus sempervirens*, to create the outlines. At the corners of each segment place matching containers. Plant these with the golden-leaved, *B. s.* 'Marginata' that can be clipped into balls. Because the balls are in containers they will appear higher than the low-growing box hedge, and give the garden vertical interest. Also, because they are evergreen, they will give the garden shape and form during winter. Planting the four borders depends on their size and your personal preference. Keep the planting as symmetrical as possible, and use plants of differing heights.

◄ *A rustic summerhouse in a formal garden, flanked by standard wisterias and tubs of lilies and auricula primulas. Euphorbias frame the steps up from the herbal knot garden.*

An informal town garden Another approach to the same basic shape involves informal curved lines, using plants and containers to alter the perspective of the garden. Map out the garden on a piece of graph paper and then make a series of curves around the edge. These will be the flower borders. Put lawn in the centre of the garden and then position a slightly winding path of stepping stones through the middle leading to a circular area where you can stand a striking container or sundial. Then place small containers where each curve joins the next. Some will not be visible from the house, or they will be partially obscured, and will therefore provide the garden with a series of secret spaces, each one highlighted by a container. Such a garden can be framed by planting one or two trees or large shrubs that initially draw the eye away from the shape of the beds, giving the whole garden an added air of mystery.

Planting a garden should vary with the seasons. Smaller spring bulbs, such as crocuses and chionodoxa, look lovely early in the year. In the early summer, colourful garden perennials, such as aquilegia and corydalis, are very useful and attractive. And, depending on the space available, do not forget smaller roses to provide colour throughout the summer, while the containers can be filled with bright summer annuals.

▶ *A monumental antique jar in a formal garden surrounded by neat low hedges of clipped box. Any unusual container or garden statue helps to draw the eye and makes a good focal point.*

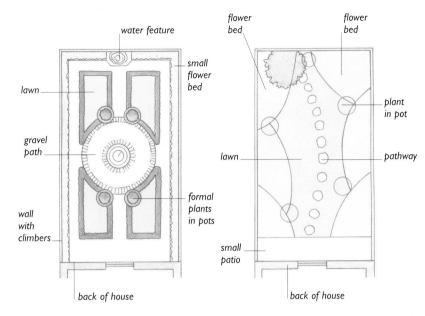

▲ *Formal and informal designs for a long town garden. The planting in the formal garden (left)* can be varied with the seasons. The informal design (right) can contain a variety of plants.*

2 3

creating rooms and features

One of the best ways to use containers is to divide one area of the garden from another. This applies just as much to large, formal gardens in the country as to small town gardens. They are an easy way to create a barrier, and if you change your mind after a season, they can always be moved.

Using containers in a small town garden

A typical small town garden has a paved area outside the back door that leads to a lawn flanked by flower beds. Two design ideas for this type of garden have been suggested on pages 22–23, but if you have a particularly long and thin garden that you want to separate into two or three divisions, then why not go even further and divide it crosswise?

To make the first division, range an even number of fairly formal containers along the edge of the patio. They do not have to block the patio from the lawn but they do create the illusion of a division, and if they are planted with colourful annuals in summer, such as petunias and lobelias, they will attract more attention. (They will also attract butterflies and bees during the hot weather.) These plants in turn make a stronger visual statement.

If there is room you could think about making a slightly raised bed at the end of the first division. Build a small retaining wall, say two or three bricks in

height, with a single step in the middle, and position four containers in front of it, two at each end, and two flanking the centre step. You can complete this design by positioning a garden seat right at the end of the garden, flanking it with a further two containers to provide a slightly formal focal point.

Containers for paths The same idea lies behind containers placed at regular intervals down a garden path, flanking the walkway rather like soldiers. This idea requires quite a large garden because, ideally, any formal path should be wide enough for two people to walk down it side by side, or for the gardener to push a loaded wheelbarrow down its length.

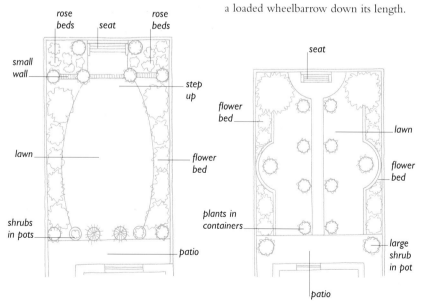

▲ *A most effective design for a larger town garden dividing the space into three 'rooms' using containers and varying levels.*

▲ *A formal garden that relies on symmetry for its effect. Matching containers flank the path down the centre of the lawn.*

◀ *Rough sketches of different areas show the number and type of container you will need. Here the gardener plans to surround a seating area with scented plants.*

❶ *Lilium* Golden Splendor
❷ *Nicotiana* Domino Mixed
❸ *Phlox* Palona Mixed
❹ *Nicotiana* Domino Mixed

Planting containers for emphasis and accent The beauty of using containers in this way is the variety that they bring to planting schemes, and the colour accents that they provide. In the summer, bright red and white pelargoniums can be planted together, or in separate containers. Blue lobelias can be included for a red, white and blue effect.

Another approach is to use the softer colours of mixed petunias in lilac, pink and white. Grey-coloured stone, concrete or fibreglass containers are an ideal foil for these paler colours, for the neutral colour of the container will blend in with the plants. Beware of using coloured containers in such positions though, because they may produce an unpleasantly jarring colour contrast.

▶ *A special display for the Chelsea Flower Show, showing sunflowers and ceanothus. Late daffodils will achieve the same colour contrast.*

containers in doors and arches

Doorways and arches are the most important points in any house or garden. The front door of a house announces the style you are aiming for. Similarly, an archway in a garden makes a statement about what is to come. It follows that any containers used need to emphasise your design.

◄ *A delightful garden with containers of hostas and dicentras and an archway of honeysuckle. Cut this back hard to keep it within bounds.*

Framing formal doorways

A much used, ever popular theme for the formal front door of a Georgian town house is two Versailles tubs, each planted with a standard bay tree, *Laurus nobilis*, clipped into a mophead. It is unnecessary to add anything else, although the trees can be mulched with stones or grey gravel to highlight the planting. Clipped box, *Buxus*, in antique terracotta pots, or spiral-shaped standards are equally good alternatives. If you want to add some colour then substitute a standard marguerite daisy, *Argyranthemum*, for its grey leaves and white flowers.

Creating a colourful welcome

In less formal surroundings with more room, you can contrive a very different effect, whether your house has a front garden or a paved area for a number of containers. In a cottage garden you can plant a climbing rose, such as the climbing form of Iceberg, which you can train over the door: its nodding white flowers are even more delicate when viewed from below. The rose can be surrounded by any number of containers planted with blue and white flowers, such as *Geranium* 'Johnson's Blue', *Lavandula angustifolia* 'Hidcote' with its dark blue flowers, complemented by white petunias or *Penstemon* 'White Bedder'. Planted in weathered terracotta pots against a matching background of brick, plants such as these provide an immediate welcome.

Formal arches

One of the most striking aspects of any garden is an archway in a formal evergreen hedge, flanked by terracotta or stone urns filled with plants of a single colour. In such cases it is almost impossible to improve on a pure white scheme, for the dark green complements the white so well, although white and blue is also very effective. Make sure that the containers suit the hedge: if you have a formal yew hedge, for example, then grand terracotta pots always look stylish.

framing a doorway

1 Measure the space around the door and then erect the trellis using battens and Rawlplugs. If you wish you can train wires instead of trellis.

2 Choose matching containers for the climbing plants and stand them on blocks to keep the containers off the ground to allow free drainage.

3 *Clematis* 'Jackmanii Superba' and *Rosa* 'Zéphirine Drouhin', the thornless rose, are good choices for a front door. They provide colour in the summer.

Planting care If you have decided to plant matching bay trees, or any formal evergreens, in pots, then you must ensure that the plants are properly pruned to shape, watered and fed. Annuals can be

changed every year and cost relatively little, but a trained standard tree is a hefty capital investment that, with care, can provide enjoyment for many years. Alternative suggestions include conifers

or even an olive tree, *Olea europaea*, which is planted in formal tubs. The latter often needs protection in the winter, and should be placed under glass during cold weather to protect it from frost.

KEEPING DOORWAY DESIGNS IN PROPORTION

One thing not to forget, when you frame the front door of a house, is the height of the door itself. Keep the container in proportion with the doorway, tall enough to make a statement, but not so tall that it is out of proportion. Try out the container, and then add the height of an imaginary plant to see what sort of effect you have achieved.
Also be certain that the style of the container matches the house. Weathered terracotta pots suit old brick cottages but formal town houses look best flanked by Versailles tubs or classical urns and planters.

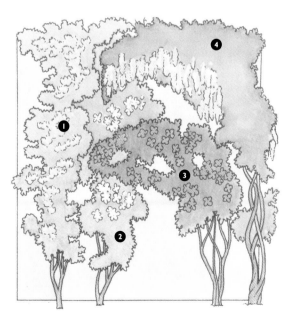

◄ *There are a number of climbers that can be used to frame doorways. Honeysuckle smells lovely but is rather untidy.* Clematis montana *is very vigorous. Wisteria is best planted in the ground and needs careful pruning.*

❶ Honeysuckle (*lonicera*)
❷ *Clematis montana*
❸ *C. 'Jackmanii Superba'*
❹ *Wisteria sinensis*

containers on steps and paths

The most dramatic use of containers is to flank formal flights of steps. Steps may lead from the semi-basement of a house to the garden or, where the garden is on several levels, they can link one area with another. Containers in these situations make a bold statement.

Matching the containers to the garden design

The first thing to consider is the style of the staircase. A narrow rustic flight built out of old bricks or wooden sleepers in a cottage garden demands small intimate containers planted to match the surroundings. A black iron fire escape or balustrade in a town garden can be brightened with red pelargoniums in terracotta pots. Informal steps leading into the house can also be decorated using climbing plants, such as clematis, planted in containers at the foot. The climbers can be tied in to the banisters, which often helps to soften what can be a harsh feature. Large stairways in grand formal gardens demand classic containers filled with matching plants, such as white hydrangeas. They draw attention to the steps and lead the walker to the next level. This is particularly true in town houses where steps lead up to the garden from a semi-basement.

▶ *Bricks make good paths, flanked here by beds with roses, foxgloves and heucheras. The container and statue add an air of mystery.*

Making use of limited space

There are many gardens where space is limited, but excellent use can be made of any steps or pathways, such as a flight of steps outside a kitchen. Culinary herbs are an excellent choice for such a position, and many will flourish in shade or partial shade. The cook has only to walk from the kitchen armed with a pair of scissors to have fresh herbs for the pot.

▶ In the summer, ordinary staircase can be disguised by containers of colourful annuals: geraniums, petunias and verbenas are all good choices.

❶ Geranium Horizon Series
❷ Verbena x hybrida
❸ Geranium Horizon Series
❹ Geranium Horizon Series
❺ Geranium Horizon Series

If you want to brighten a dull passageway, for example a side passage next to a town house, then this too is possible, but if you are growing flowering plants that need sun, make sure that you rotate the containers so that the plants regularly get bright light. If you just use a few sun-loving plants as accents the task need not be too onerous.

Containers along passageways

Remember that there is likely to be more light in a passageway the higher up the wall you go. The maximum shade is usually at ground level. There may well be a case for using wall pots positioned on the wall, especially if it catches some sun. Another advantage is that space can be left for pedestrians, bicycles and children's toys. There must also be room to walk down flights of stairs easily, especially fire escapes, and you can only place containers on steps or walkways if they leave excellent access.

Aspect – sun and shade

When you are planning and planting your containers you must always remember the aspect. Containers placed in south-facing positions that are in the sun a lot can get very hot. Grow plants that will flourish in hot dry conditions: any plant, such as lavender or rosemary, that comes from the Mediterranean will do well. Similarly, north-facing and shaded areas need plants that will survive in shade with low light levels. Suitable plants are listed on pages 88–89.

▲ A wrought-iron spiral staircase looks good in a small garden with different levels: lupins, foxgloves and lilies add colour in the summer.

▲ Cactus plants can be put outside in the summer months. The blue-grey leaves make a good background for the scarlet geraniums.

29

colour schemes
in containers

*Choosing plants that harmonize with each other as well as with their backgrounds is important,
especially when trying to create the best display in a small area. Some colours, such as red and rich
orange are hot colours and therefore dramatic. Cool colours, such as white and pale blue, are more
restful and can be used in larger groups than hot colours. While yellow flowers especially appeal to
children and those rich in original thinking and vitality.*

creating a colour scheme

Most garden colour schemes work reasonably well. The green leaves help to give an overall balance and white and pale flowers link the stronger colours. But rather than leaving everything to chance, it is better to plan definite colour schemes. This is especially important in a small container garden.

The colour wheel

Colour theory is based on the colour wheel. An understanding of how this works explains the relationship between colours, and helps the gardener to achieve balanced plantings.

Primary colours The three primary colours are red, yellow and blue. They cannot be obtained, in a painter's palette, by mixing other colours together. Mixtures of the primary colours,

▲ *A colour wheel composed of plants, showing the primary and secondary colours. Check to see which colour combination you prefer.*

together with black and white, produce virtually all the other colours available. In gardening terms the primary colours fit together quite nicely. For example you could plant a spring container with forget-me-not, *Myosotis*, primrose, *Primula vulgaris* and a few early tulips, such as 'Brilliant Star', scarlet-vermilion, or 'Tornado', scarlet-red. They would all flower together in early to mid-spring, and the effect would be bright and cheerful. If you wanted a quieter scheme you could leave out the tulips and just have the blue and yellow of the forget-me-nots and primroses. The forget-me-nots are important because they provide the groundcover necessary for this type of planting.

Later in the year beds or containers based on the primary colours might contain red and yellow celosias with blue cornflower, *Centaurea cyanus* – the variety 'Dwarf Blue' only reaches 30cm/12in and is suitable for containers. You might find these colours too strong in midsummer because the shades are deeper than the spring planting, and

colours appear brighter in the summer months than they do earlier in the year. when the sun is lower in the sky. The effect would be vivid rather than restful.

Secondary and complementary colours
If you mix any two primary colours in varying quantities you will obtain a secondary colour. Red and blue make purple, red and yellow make orange, and blue and yellow make green.

Complementary colours are those that lie opposite one another on the colour wheel, and in theory if you mix two of them you should obtain a pale grey, although if you try this with paint the pigments are seldom pure enough for this to happen. If you add white to a colour this produces a tint, and if you add black this produces a shade.

Adding combinations of both black and white produces a number of tonal values. These tonal values are most important for the gardener and the planning of planting schemes, and the best combination of plants is where there is a tonal harmony in the planting.

◀ A red, yellow and orange scheme
for the autumn can be created with
a variety of dahlias and day lilies
with low-growing scarlet begonias in
front and taller red crocosmia plants
at the rear. This produces a good
blend of colours that is strong but
not too vibrant.

① *Crocosmia* 'Lucifer'

② *Dahlia* 'Bishop of Llandaff'

③ *Begonia* 'Barcos'

④ *Dahlia* Unwins Dwarf Group

⑤ *Hemerocallis* 'Bertie Ferris'

⑥ *Hemerocallis* 'Lusty Lealand'

⑦ *Dahlia* 'Hugh Mather'

⑧ *Dahlia* Unwins Dwarf Group

⑨ *Dahlia* 'Jeanette Carter'

The effect of various plantings

Plantings based on the hot colours, red,
yellow and orange, are vivid and striking
while the cooler colours are more
restful. The same goes for the various
shades. Pale colours blend softly together
and are easy to live with.

All plant groupings in a small
container garden need to be planned so
that they fit in with the house and its
surroundings. The walls of the house and
garden may well be built of brick in
various colours. New red bricks may not
make the best background for plants.
One solution might be to paint the
inside of the garden walls white, but a
longer term plan might be to grow ivy
in a container to cover it. Green foliage
is often the best foil for flowers.

▶ Plantings of primary colours, such as red and
yellow, certainly catch the eye, but the general
effect can be a bit hot and restless.

hot planting schemes

Brightly coloured plants from the hot section of the colour wheel achieve instant effect whether in a border or a container. Hot schemes need to be planned with care because the effect can be unsettling unless the colour is controlled. Such plantings can be softened with white or pale flowers.

Hot schemes with red and yellow bulbs

The most important red and yellow bulbs are tulips and daffodils, *Narcissus*. They do not really flower at the same time with the daffodils coming first. If you want to try to achieve simultaneous flowering, you need to read the catalogues carefully and choose tulips from Division 1 – Single Early Group, Division 12 – Kaufmanniana Group or Division 14 – the Greigii Group. These groups all flower relatively early in spring. Tulips have a complicated classification and there are 15 divisions in all. Daffodils are almost equally complicated and have 11 divisions. Those that flower latest are varieties from Division 5 – Triandrus, Division 7 – Jonquilla and Division 9 – Poeticus. In general gardening terms most people refer to flowers from all these groups as *Narcissus*. In fact dwarf narcissus are very suitable for containers and there are

▲ *An attractive spring container of red, blue and yellow flowers. Choose small tulips from the Kaufmanniana or Greigii groups.*

many good varieties. *N. cyclamineus* 'February Gold', *N. c.* 'April Tears' and *N. c.* 'Peeping Tom' are all clear yellow, while *N. c.* 'Andalusia' is a typical narcissus, with yellow petals and a strong orange-coloured cup.

There are many red, yellow and orange tulips. Among the best for the container gardener are the smaller varieties, such as *Tulipa praestans* 'Fusilier', 'Red Riding Hood' and 'Cantata', all red; *T. linifolia* Batalinii Group 'Bright Gem' and 'Yellow Gem' yellow; and *T.* 'Love Song' and 'Shakespeare', orange. If you want to combine two hot colours in one flower, *T. clusiana* var. *chrysantha* is red and yellow, and 'Stresa' is gold with red on the outer petals.

◄ *A brilliant hot arrangement of annuals. The whole effect is softened by the white petunias that emphasise the startling reds and purples.*

You can plan a most effective hot planting scheme using different varieties of tulips, each in its own container. Choose tulips from the same division to ensure, as far as possible, that they flower at the same time to make the most impact. And if you do not want just red and yellow then you can choose any number of colour combinations.

Hot-coloured bulbs and tubers for summer schemes

Other red bulbs or corms you might consider for the container garden include *Crocosmia* 'Lucifer', red, and *C.* 'Golden Fleece', yellow, although crocosmia reach 1–1.2m/3–4ft in height and will probably need staking. Day lilies, *Hemerocallis*, are more suitable for they are smaller. The varieties 'Red Joy', 'Red Rum' and 'Stafford' are red; 'Golden Chimes', 'Little Rainbow' and 'Nova' are yellow; and 'Francis Joiner' and *H. fulva* 'Flore Pleno' are orange. Day lilies flower in midsummer; some varieties are evergreen and continue to add interest during the months of winter.

A hot scheme of dahlias

The other excellent tuber for the dedicated container gardener is the dahlia. Dahlias should be lifted when the first frosts arrive in the autumn, and be stored in a frost-free environment over winter. They are ideal plants to alternate with tulips if you want to produce a hot colour scheme in late spring, and again in late summer in the same container. Lift the tulips when flowering is over

and keep them in a spare container until the foliage has died down, then store and replant the bulbs in the autumn. Plant out the dahlia tubers in late spring or early summer after the tulips are over. Hot-coloured dahlias include 'Bishop of Llandaff', 'Christopher Taylor' and 'Rothesay Superb', all red; 'Hans Ricken' 'Lady Sunshine' and 'Ruskin Diane', all yellow; and 'Gateshead Festival' and 'Highgate Torch', both orange, but there are many thousands of varieties to choose from. All those mentioned will reach 1–1.2m/3–4ft high and require staking. Dwarf bedding dahlias are usually grown as annuals.

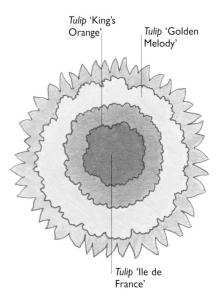

Tulip 'King's Orange'

Tulip 'Golden Melody'

Tulip 'Ile de France'

▲ *A hot colour wheel of tulips looks spectacular but it has to be planned and planted with care. The trouble with tulips is that there are a number of divisions, many with different shaped flower-heads, different heights, and all flowering at different times.*

◀ *'Paul's Lemon Pillar' is a popular climbing rose that is often trained up pergolas. The flowers are double, white, with a lemon scent.*

Red and yellow clematis

If you want to grow a climber but do not want to plant a rose try a clematis. There are not that many with red and yellow flowers because most are white or varying shades of blue and violet, but of the larger-flowered varieties there are 'Guernsey Cream', creamy yellow, and 'Horn of Plenty', 'Niobe', 'Sealand Gem', 'Ville de Lyon' and 'Vino', differing shades of red. These all flower from midsummer onwards. Of the smaller-flowered varieties there are *C. alpina* 'Ruby', red; *C. macropetala* 'Rosy O'Grady', deep pink; and *C. viticella* 'Madame Julia Correvon', wine-red. The best yellow clematis are *C. orientalis* and *C. tangutica*. The last two flower from late summer into autumn.

Hot schemes for midsummer containers – climbers and perennials

Red and orange flowers in containers in the summer must inevitably revolve around annuals and bedding plants. Red geraniums would be a popular first choice, closely followed by busy Lizzie, *Impatiens*. However, larger containers can support larger plants, and when planning a planting scheme in a container garden it is a good idea to use some of these as highlights.

Climbers for the container garden

The favourite climber is the rose – if you can, plant a climbing rose and train it against a wall. Most will flourish perfectly well in containers provided they are fed properly. There are two things to look out for but first check how much sun it will receive, and then how much room have you got. Do not choose a rose, such as an old-fashioned rambler, because it will rapidly outgrow the confines of the container garden, and you need to make sure you have room to walk around it. Also only the pink rose 'Zéphirine Drouhin' is completely thornless. Climbing roses for a hot colour scheme include 'Ena Harkness', scarlet; 'Etoile de Hollande' and 'Parkdirektor Riggers', deep crimson; 'Golden Showers', golden-yellow and suitable for a north wall; 'Maigold', yellow-orange and suitable for a north wall; 'Paul Lédé', buff yellow; and 'Paul's Lemon Pillar', paler yellow.

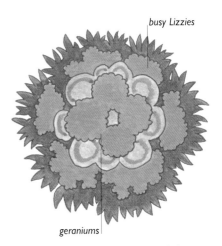

busy Lizzies

geraniums

▲ *Red geraniums can be surrounded by busy Lizzies but schemes of this type can be softened by including white and pink varieties.*

Two yellow wall shrubs

If you have large enough containers and want a background for a hot colour scheme, there are two rather unusual yellow wall shrubs that you might consider: *Fremontodendron* 'Californian Glory' and pineapple broom, *Cytisus battandieri*. Both need a south or south-west wall and a good deal of sun. Otherwise, to vary the colour schemes during the seasons, a firethorn, *Pyracantha*, could be planted in a raised bed and trained against a wall. It is prickly and evergreen, and a good guard against intruders. It has white flowers in late spring but the chief glory is the clusters of bright red, or red and orange berries that follow in the autumn. They last the whole winter untouched by the birds.

Japonica, *Chaenomeles speciosa*, and its varieties also have thorny stems: they carry red flowers on bare branches in early spring, while *Abutilon megapotamicum* is evergreen and bears drooping red and yellow flowers through the summer.

Once you have decided on the climber or wall shrub that you want, you can consider the rest of the planting scheme. It would be a mistake to plant the hot-coloured red-hot poker, *Kniphofia*, in a container. It takes up too much room and spreads endlessly. Also avoid the brilliant red poppies for they last such a short time in flower, but *Rudbeckia laciniata* 'Goldquelle' is reasonably compact with clear yellow daisy-like, multi-petalled flowerheads, and there is no red in the garden like *Salvia splendens,* which is a must.

Rose 'Golden Showers'

Rose 'Ena Harkness'

▲ *If you have room plant two climbing roses together. 'Golden Showers' is a free-flowering yellow rose, 'Climbing Ena Harkness' is red.*

▼ *The clematis 'Mme Julia Correvon' flowers from midsummer to late autumn. The wine-red flowers are single with yellow stamens.*

cool planting schemes

Blue and white are the colours for cool planting schemes, and they can be complemented by adding grey and silver-leaved plants. They help to make any garden a calm and restful place in summer. Pale colour schemes can be used to link stronger schemes and look best against a dark background.

Using blue and white plants

Blue plants can be used in a number of ways. In a traditional garden border, blue flowers, such as anchusas or dark blue delphiniums, can be used to contrast with the vivid red poppies, *Papaver.* In late spring red tulips might be planted amongst a bed of grape hyacinths, *Muscari.* These contrasting primary colours are very effective, but a garden full of such colour contrasts would not be a restful place. In the confines of a container garden space is at a premium so avoid such luxuries.

In the early months of the year blue and white schemes are easy to create using bulbs. For example, a container planted with alternate blue and white hyacinths, *Hyacinthus,* looks and smells wonderful, but they will probably need some form of staking to keep them upright. Or include some other plants.

Winter-flowering heathers, *Erica carnea* and *E. x darleyensis,* have a number of white forms, and white *Erica* can be planted in containers with blue and purple crocuses, such as *Crocus chrysanthus* 'Blue Pearl', *C. c.* 'Ladykiller', *C. tommasinianus* and *C. vernus* 'Pickwick' – all flower at the time when winter seems never-ending and are doubly welcome. If you do not want to go to the trouble of filling a container with ericaceous compost, necessary if *Erica* is to flower at its best, then other blue and white bulb combinations could include glory-of-the-snow, *Chionodoxa luciliae* Gigantea Group – *C. gigantea* is blue with white stripes, and *C. g. alba* is white.

If you have a larger container and would like to expand the range of plants to cover a larger canvas, then you can add some small conifers, such as *Chamaecyparis lawsoniana* 'Barry's Silver', green with silvery-white tips on the new

Erica x *darleyensis* 'White Perfection'

Crocus 'Blue Pearl'

Crocus 'Pickwick'

Viola x *wittrockiana* 'True Blue'

Viola 'Joker Light Blue'

Iris 'Joyce'

Erica x *darleyensis* 'White Glow'

◄ *A charming mixture of spring-flowering plants. Substitute V. 'Blue Shades' or 'Lavender Shades' if individual varieties are unavailable.*

shoots in summer; *Picea glauca* 'Alberta Blue', smoky grey-blue; or *Juniperus communis* 'Compressa', green and found in many a rock garden. They all provide permanent colour and form. Miniature daffodils, *Narcissus*, such as 'Peeping Tom', which is a yellow variety, add a touch of sunlight and can be planted in small groups with similar narcissus with contrasting colours that will flower at the same time. 'Trena' has white petals and bright yellow long trumpets, while 'Jenny' is almost pure white.

Blue-flowering bulbs that flower at roughly the same time include glory-of-the-snow, *Chionodoxa*, and *Scilla sibirica*. Grape hyacinths, *Muscari*, flower slightly later. Alternatively plant some of the bulbous *Reticulata* irises that flower in late winter and early spring – 'Harmony' and 'Joyce' have striking blue flowers with a splash of yellow.

Clumps of *Alyssum spinosum* and *Iberis saxatilis* continue the white theme into early summer, and can be intermingled with the brilliant blue of aubretia, *Aubrieta*, planted so that it falls over the front of the container. The only problem with such an arrangement is the straggly foliage when the flowering is over. Since bulbs absorb their strength from the foliage as it dies down you either have to live with this or, more extravagantly, dig up the bulbs and replant with new ones in the autumn.

▶ A deep purple, pale yellow, cream, white, green and silver grouping of annuals frames an old chimney in a small garden.

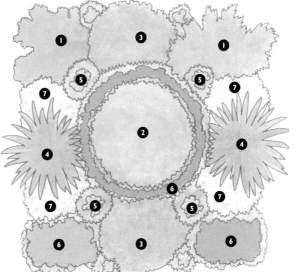

◀ Conifers are the basis of this green. blue and yellow arrangement that looks good all year.

1 Cedrus deodora 'Feelin' Blue'
2 Chamaecyparis lawsoniana
3 Picea pungens 'Globosa'
4 Thuja orientalis 'Raffles'
5 Narcissus 'Peeping Tom'
6 Muscari armeniacum
7 Iberis saxatilis

blue and white schemes

Blue and white planting schemes, often mixed with yellow, are most successful in the spring before the annuals come into flower. All container gardeners should try one. Similar herbaceous border schemes later in the year include blue delphiniums or hardy geraniums grown against a background of the honey-scented, billowing white of the 2.1m/7ft high *Crambe cordifolia*, blue and white irises that complement each other and, as summer comes to an end, blue, purple and white Michaelmas daisies, *Aster novi-belgii*, to provide a restraining influence on the golden colours of autumn. The container gardener, however, will have difficulty growing such plants effectively because they either take up too much room or have too large roots, and in almost all cases such attempts are doomed to failure.

Using African lilies

There are, nevertheless, a number of ideas that are worth considering. If you have a sunny garden or patio and a mild climate, consider planting a container with *Agapanthus*, African lily. They are ideal container plants, although they require staking. The best and hardiest are the Headbourne Hybrids that are widely available. 'Bressingham Blue', another popular hybrid, is a deep violet colour. Surround the agapanthus with two matching containers, lower in height, and plant one of the lovely white rock roses, *Cistus*, in each. *Cistus* x *cyprius* is justifiably popular, each petal marked with a maroon blotch in the centre, while *Cistus* x *corbariensis* has clear white petals and yellow stamens. Rock roses will flower before agapanthus, through early to late summer.

◀ *Mauve petunias, verbena and salvias are emphasised by white daisies. Take care when placing flowers against a dark background.*

▶ *Agapanthus make good container plants. Headbourne Hybrids are popular blue forms, 'Bressingham White' is white.*

Consider hardy geraniums

Another colourful scheme would be to take a selection of the smaller hardy geraniums and group them together. Cranesbills, *Geranium*, are a large genus and some are quite unsuitable for the container gardener because they grow too tall and are too vigorous, but some of the smaller ones are among the most charming and rewarding plants in any garden, flowering for months on end. The main difficulty is trying to group those that flower at the same time because they have rather different time clocks. *Geranium wallichianum* 'Buxton's Variety' is deservedly popular, its petals sky-blue on the outside and white veined within. However it can be difficult to find in ordinary nurseries, and it flowers rather late in the year from late summer into early autumn. *Geranium clarkei* 'Kashmir Blue' has soft pale-blue flowers and *G. c.* 'Kashmir White' is

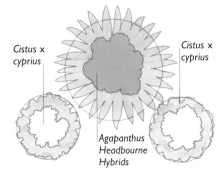

Cistus ×
cyprius

Cistus ×
cyprius

Agapanthus
Headbourne
Hybrids

▲ *An easy way to group colours is to grow one variety of plant in each container. Move them around until you have the right colour balance.*

white with thin pink veins on the petals. Neither is too vigorous and they flower early in the summer months.

Other suitable white geraniums for containers include *G. sanguineum* 'Album', white flowers throughout the summer; *G. renardii*, white to pale-lavender flowers with strong violet veins on the petals in early summer; and *G. pratense* 'Striatum', somewhat larger, with white flowers streaked with blue in midsummer. These white varieties can all be mixed with any of the lovely violet-blue forms, such as *G.* 'Johnson's Blue', the most popular geranium of all. The whole design can be further warmed by the addition of one of the wonderful pink varieties, such as *G. c.* 'Kashmir Pink'.

A blue and white scheme in summer can be mixed with climbers. White climbing roses suitable for a small space include the slow-growing 'White Cockade', delicately scented with small, perfect tea-shaped flowers, or more vigorous 'Swan Lake', white flowers that have a touch of pink in the centre.

Large-flowered white clematis that flower from midsummer onwards include *C.* 'Henryi', 'James Mason' and 'John Huxtable', and attractive blue forms include 'General Sikorski', 'H.F. Young' and the ever-popular 'Jackmanii Superba', although there are many other kinds available. They can create a cool space in a summer garden and make it both restful and pleasurable.

pale pink and red schemes

Hot and cool schemes may look well in isolation and garden designers can achieve spectacular effects with them, but a mixture of shades is still the most popular plan for ordinary gardeners. The secret is to combine plants to provide constant colour and a changing emphasis throughout the year.

▲ *A pink and red spring mixture of pansies, heather and ranunculus. The clipped box provides a pleasing green background.*

The effect of white flowers

There are two points to bear in mind. The first is the blending effect that white plants have on other colours. Red, blue and yellow plants all work well together if there are white plants in between, and the use of white also strengthens the other colours and makes them more effective. The other main point is to try and include one plant with a stronger colour impact, for instance a group of pale pink flowers might look slightly anaemic, a dark red rose in the middle gives the whole design more purpose.

Various colour combinations work particularly well especially those from the same quarter of the colour wheel – blue, pink and white are one good combination and you can add some yellow plants for contrast provided that the yellow is not too strong and it matches the tones of the blues. Cream and pale orange flowers are equally effective. Another good colour combination includes various shades of red through to pink, and another green,

white and yellow. The main points are to match the general tone of each plant.

Certain colour combinations are easier to achieve at different times of the year. Blue and yellow flowers are easy to find during the early months of the year but there are very few pink and red flowers in bloom. In the summer, pink, mauve, red and white flowers often predominate and are easy to group together. The container gardener is also limited by the suitability of the various plants and this has to be born in mind.

A pink, white and red scheme for the spring garden

One of the best small trees to grow in a container is a camellia, and one of the pink, white or red varieties can be the starting point for a pink-based spring planting scheme. Camellias prefer a shady site, and their shiny dark green leaves remain attractive when the flowers have faded and fallen. Although some varieties will tolerate lime in the soil, the majority need acid soil, and therefore if you would like to grow a camellia and you have alkaline soil, a container filled with ericaceous compost is the only way you will achieve success. Ideally you should also try to collect and use rainwater because tap water may well contain lime. Alternatively sprinkle the compost with sulphur powder or add sulphur chips to keep the compost at the right pH level.

There are large numbers of suitable camellias and they come from two main groups, the *japonica* hybrids and the x *williamsii* hybrids. Eventually plants from both groups will grow too large for a container, but they are slow-growing shrubs and can be pruned back quite hard when they threaten to outgrow their surrounds. Pink camellias include 'Akashigata' ('Lady Clare'), 'Apple Blossom', 'Inspiration', 'Ave Maria', 'Lady Loch', 'Lasca Beauty' and 'Spring Festival'. White varieties include 'Cornish Snow', 'Gauntlettii' ('Lotus'), 'White Swan' and 'Devonia'. The red ones include 'Adolphe Audusson', 'R L Wheeler', 'Lady de Sausmarez' and 'Royalty'. A pleasant scheme for the early spring might include three camellias in separate containers underplanted with white *Anemone blanda* 'White Splendour', or the pink form *A. b.* 'Charmer'. Other low-growing plants include varieties of *Primula allionii*. They vary in colour from white to pink to reddish-purple; *P. vulgaris* 'Alba Plena' is white, and the long-flowering *P.* 'Wanda' is deep red.

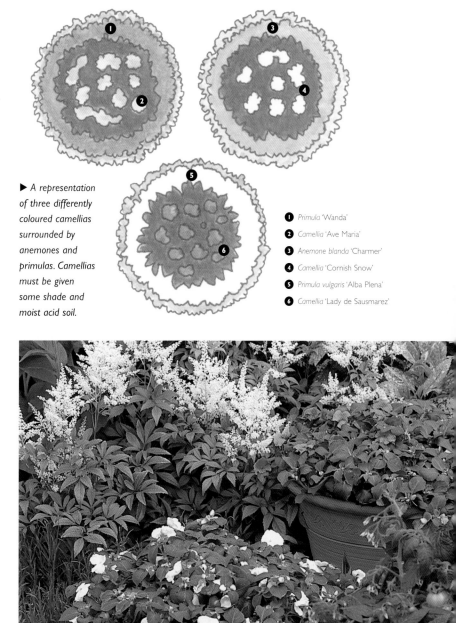

▶ A representation of three differently coloured camellias surrounded by anemones and primulas. Camellias must be given some shade and moist acid soil.

❶ Primula 'Wanda'
❷ Camellia 'Ave Maria'
❸ Anemone blanda 'Charmer'
❹ Camellia 'Cornish Snow'
❺ Primula vulgaris 'Alba Plena'
❻ Camellia 'Lady de Sausmarez'

▶ A most imaginative arrangement of white and mauve busy Lizzies against a background of white astilbes growing in a raised bed.

seasonal ideas

Containers can be drenched in colour throughout the year. Window boxes are planned to be awash with flowers throughout summer, while in early autumn the display can be changed to include young and small evergreen shrubs with variegated leaves, or miniature conifers with coloured foliage. Hanging baskets are at their best during summer when packed with a combination of bushy and trailing plants. Large containers are best suited for dominant herbaceous perennials, slow-growing conifers and small shrubs.

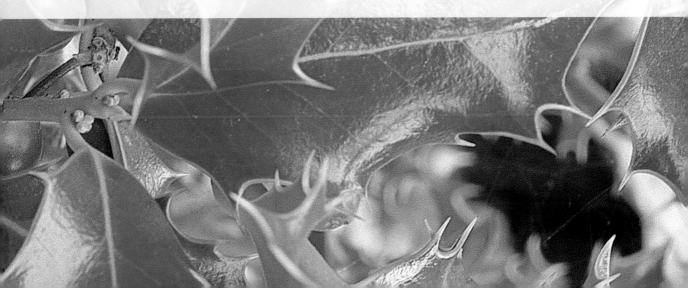

container gardening in winter

Many plants are suitable for a container garden in winter: evergreens, shrubs with berries, winter-flowering shrubs, early spring bulbs, and most importantly, winter-flowering annuals or biennials. It is best to confine them to one or two containers, leaving room for the plants of spring and summer.

Evergreens for the winter garden – conifers

The most popular, and most suitable, evergreen trees for containers are conifers. They offer a choice of colours,

blue-grey, green and yellow-green, and many are dwarf, only reaching a height of 1.8m/6ft or less over a period of years. However, if you are particularly fond of the colouring of other conifers, it is worth checking on their growth rate with a reputable conifer nursery. While many are scheduled to reach a height of 12–15m/40–50ft in optimum conditions in open gardens, they can grow very slowly and will only reach 3m/10ft after 10 years. If they grow too large too fast, then they can always be removed. This applies to the lovely blue conifers *Picea pungens* 'Koster' and *Chamaecyparis lawsoniana* 'Pembury Blue', both popular choices in a number of gardens. Playing safe, the following dwarf conifers are worth considering: Upright conical trees – *Juniperus communis* 'Compressa', green; *J. c.* 'Gold Cone' and 'Golden Showers', golden yellow; and *J. c.* 'Hibernica', grey-green. Low-growing spreading trees – *J.* x *media* 'Gold Sovereign', yellow; *J.* x *m.* 'Pfitzeriana', green; and *J. horizontalis* 'Douglasii', blue-grey.

Rounded conical trees – *Chamaecyparis lawsoniana* 'Barry's Silver', silver-grey; *C. l.* 'Minima', green; *Taxus baccata* 'Aurea' and *Thuja plicata* 'Collyer's Gold', both golden yellow.

Evergreen and winter-flowering shrubs

There are a number of these, including: *Camellia japonica* and *C.* x *williamsii* hybrids. Attractive evergreen small trees or shrubs, camellias have glossy evergreen leaves and gorgeous multi-petalled flowers, generally red, pink or white. They are slow growing, and can be pruned back quite hard when they threaten to outgrow their space (you do lose some flowers). They need at least semi-shade and acid soil to flourish. Pink camellias include 'Akashigata' ('Lady Clare'), 'Apple Blossom', 'Inspiration', 'Ave Maria', 'Lady Loch', 'Lasca Beauty' and 'Spring Festival'. White varieties include 'Cornish Snow', 'Gauntlettii' ('Lotus'), 'White Swan' and 'Devonia'. And red ones include 'Adolphe Audusson' and 'R L Wheeler'.

▲ *Conifers are among the best plants for the winter. There are yellow, blue and green varieties, and many change colour throughout the year.*

Daphne: this is a group of deciduous and evergreen shrubs that are noted for their heavily scented flowers. The following are worth considering – *Daphne cneorum,* evergreen with rose-pink flowers in late spring; *D. mezereum*, deciduous, with heavily scented pink to purple flowers in late winter and early spring; and *D. odorata*, evergreen, with very fragrant flowers in winter and early spring but it is not fully hardy.

Elaeagnus x *ebbingei* and its cultivars are evergreen and grown for their yellow and green-splashed leaves. They have small white, rather insignificant flowers in the autumn. Eventually they will grow too large for a container garden and have to be replaced, although this will take some time.

Erica carnea and *E.* x *darleyensis*. The winter-flowering heathers are great stand-bys for the winter container gardener. They prefer acid soil, although there are some varieties that tolerate alkaline soil provided it is not too limy. The colours range from white through pink to a deep purple-pink. The varieties *E. c.* 'Springwood Pink' and 'Springwood White' both trail and are suitable for covering the fronts of window boxes.

Firethorns, *Pyracantha*, make excellent evergreen wall shrubs whose only disadvantage is the long spikes that grow on the branches. Their chief glory is the berries, red, orange and yellow,

▶ *Some dwarf conifers are very small indeed and grow remarkably slowly. They are suitable for small containers.*

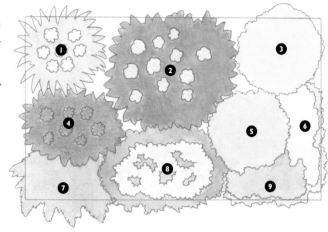

◀ *A group of winter-flowering shrubs.*

1. *Camellia* 'Cornish Snow'
2. *Camellia* 'Apple Blossom'
3. *Elaeagnus* x *ebbingei*
4. *Camellia* 'RL Wheeler'
5. *Daphne cneorum*
6. *Erica carnea* 'Springwood Pink'
7. *Daphne odorata*
8. *Erica carnea* 'December Red'
9. *Erica carnea* 'Vivelli'

according to the variety grown, that stay on the plants throughout the winter. In the spring they carry white flowers.

Skimmia japonica is another evergreen shrub, and the variety 'Bowles' Dwarf' is small and compact (male and female plants are needed to produce flowers and fruit). 'Rubella' is a compact male clone. Skimmias have bright red berries that last throughout the winter.

◄ *Helleborus lividus has beautiful green flowers early in the year. All hellebores are poisonous and should be handled with care.*

being grown, and the flowers are often marked with spots and veins on the inside. They like a degree of shade and some, such as stinking hellebore, *H. foetidus*, will flourish in deep shade.

Iris unguicularis is the winter-flowering rhizomatous iris that produces blue-purple flowers on short stalks early in the year. The sedge-like leaves are evergreen. It is a good plant for a single container because otherwise it spreads too freely. After 3–5 years split and replant the rhizomes, discarding the portions from the centre.

Early bulbs

Early snowdrop, *Galanthus* spp., will flower at the beginning of the New Year, with the main flowering period being the following month. (In the northern hemisphere their common name used to be Fair Maids of February.) Lovely as

Clematis cirrhosa is an evergreen climber with green leaves, bronze underneath. Small cup-shaped cream flowers appear in late winter and early spring. The variety *balearica* has fragrant cream flowers with red speckles inside, and 'Freckles' has creamy pink flowers that are similarly heavily speckled.

Ivy, *Hedera*, creates a permanent background in a container garden, and the best ivies to grow are varieties of Canary ivy, *H. canariensis*, although they may suffer in hard winters, or common ivy, *H. helix*; *H. c.* 'Gloire de Marengo' has gold-splashed leaves, *H. h.* 'Anne Marie' has leaves with white margins, and *H. h.* 'Atropurpurea' has bronzy leaves. Many other varieties are available in varying shades of green.

Winter jasmine, *Jasminum nudiflorum*, is an excellent wall shrub that does not climb, cling or twine and therefore needs to be tied in. It is grown for the long pendent green shoots and the bright yellow flowers that appear before the leaves in late winter and early spring. Cut out dead wood, and shorten flowering shoots by a third after flowering.

Winter flowering plants

The Christmas rose, *Helleborus niger*, and the Lenten rose, *H. orientalis*, are both slightly misnamed because they seldom appear exactly when the name suggests. Putting that quibble aside, they are wonderful winter plants with bold clumps of flowers, white, pink, creamy yellow or green, according to the kind

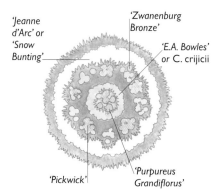

'Jeanne d'Arc' or 'Snow Bunting'
'Zwanenburg Bronze'
'E.A. Bowles' or C. crijicii
'Pickwick'
'Purpureus Grandiflorus'

▲ *You can make a colour wheel of crocuses, varying the colours according to your taste. Plant them thickly for maximum impact.*

► A grouping of climbers and containers that will give flowers in the early part of the year. Winter jasmine flowers on bare branches and needs to be pruned after flowering.

❶ *Clematis cirrhosa 'Freckles'*

❷ *Jasminum nudiflorum*

❸ *Hellebore argustifolius*

❹ *Crocus 'Queen of the Blues'*

❺ *Iris unguicularis*

❻ *Hedera helix 'Anne Marie'*

❼ *Crocus vernus*

they are it is doubtful whether they are really suitable for a container garden because they should have been planted when they were in leaf the previous year, and then left through the summer for the leaves to die down until they spring to life again in the middle of winter. If you want to grow snowdrops, plant them quite deeply in a container with small groups of crocus bulbs.

Crocuses are much easier than snowdrops, and can be planted early in the autumn to flower the following spring. Some of the best are varieties of Dutch crocus, *C. vernus*. Look out for 'Pickwick', lilac-striped; 'Jeanne d'Arc', white and purple; 'Vanguard', pale lilac; and *C. chrysanthus* hybrids such as 'E.A. Bowles', gold and bronze; 'Snow

Bunting', white; and 'Gipsy Girl', yellow and purple. There are many available.

Winter aconite, *Eranthis hyemalis*, is a tuberous perennial that will make large clumps in alkaline soil, so do not grow it in any container with acid compost. The yellow flowers open just after the first snowdrops, and when they flower together they make a lovely picture signifying the approach of spring.

Finally, there are the winter annuals. The best flowers are provided by a number of the winter-flowering primulas that appear in so many bright colours, and the winter-flowering pansy, *Viola* x *wittrockiana*. Every garden should have some containers planted with them because they flower from early autumn right through the winter into the spring.

▼ A number of the smaller irises make excellent plants in a container in early spring. This vigorous variety is I. histrioides 'Major' that has beautiful deep-blue flowers.

container gardening in spring

Spring is one of the loveliest times of the year in the garden but the container gardener needs to plan carefully. Space is often limited and containers that will be filled with summer annuals or vegetables need to be empty and prepared to receive the summer plants.

Spring-flowering bulbs

Most people associate spring with bulbs. Daffodils and narcissus are everybody's favourite but there are many other bulbs that are suitable for the container garden. They include tulips, scillas, grape hyacinth, *Muscari*, hyacinth, *Hyacinthus*, glory-of-the-snow, *Chionodoxa*, and dog-toothed violet, *Erythronium*. With a little trouble you can create a considerable display of spring bulbs in a small container by taking advantage of the differing sizes of the bulbs. The container needs to have been planted early in the autumn the previous year, and planned with care. Plant the largest bulbs, the daffodils, at the bottom, and then plant other bulbs in layers with the smallest at the top. All bulbs should be covered at least two and a half times their height with soil. The large bulbs will grow between the smaller ones, and the

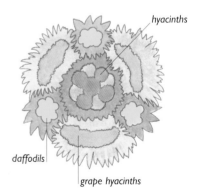

hyacinths

daffodils

grape hyacinths

▲ *An arrangement of primary colours for late spring. This type of selection can be brightened by adding white and orange narcissi.*

◄ *The deep, deep purple of these 'Black Swan' tulips recalls the tulipomania of the 18th century. 'Recreado' is another deep-purple one.*

◀ *Narcissus 'Tête-à-Tête' is a popular bulb for containers and makes a good display indoors. Plant in the autumn for early spring flowering.*

although not all are suitable for growing in containers, a number are. Plan carefully because much depends on how much room is available, and what you intend growing in the summer.

Some of the best flowering shrubs are those that flower early in the year, notably camellias and pieris. They both require acid soil with camellias needing partial shade, and pieris full sun or partial shade. The attraction of pieris is the new red leaves and bunches of white flowers. The most commonly grown are varieties of *Pieris japonica*. Both pieris and camellias grow slowly enough to be included in a container garden.

Another lovely spring-flowering shrub that does not grow too quickly is the pearl bush, *Exochorda* x *macrantha* 'The Bride'. It prefers neutral or slightly acid soil, and has waterfalls of white flowers that hang from the branches.

container will produce a succession of flowers. It may be difficult to plan for them all to flower together. There are many varieties of daffodils and tulips, all with different flowering periods. Broadly speaking the daffodils flower before the tulips, the scillas and chionodoxa flower at roughly the same time, just after the crocuses and before the daffodils, while grape hyacinths, hyacinths and dog-toothed violets flower a few weeks later.

❶ *Scilla siberica*
❷ *Muscari armeniaca*
❸ *Chionodoxa luciliae*
❹ *Narcissus*
❺ *Hyacinthus 'China Pink, 'L'Innocence'*
❻ *Tulip kaufmanniana*
❼ *Erythronium 'Pagoda'*
❽ *Erythronium revolutum*

▶ *Containers of spring bulbs that will come into flower one after another. They can include tulips, grape hyacinths and daffodils.*

Spring-flowering shrubs

When confronted with the question 'What should I plant to flower in spring?', many a gardener finds it difficult to come up with anything beyond spring bulbs and forsythia. However, there are many shrubs that flower in spring and

pink; 'Ruby', red with white stamens; and 'White Columbine', white. *Macropetala* varieties are very similar to *alpina*s but look as if they have double flowers because they have inner stamens shaped like petals. The best known include 'Blue Bird', 'Markham's Pink', 'Rosy O'Grady' and 'White Swan'.

The fruit blossom of spring

In Japan they have a festival of spring, devoted to the blossom of the cherry tree. There are few container gardens with the room to grow individual ornamental cherry trees, and even the upright *Prunus* 'Amanogawa' will eventually grow too tall and large, but fruit trees trained against a wall or fence are possible. The blossom they carry in

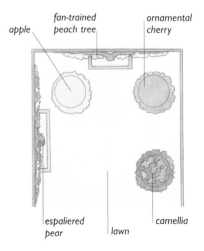

A small garden can take fruit trees in containers, as shown in this plan. Make sure there is plenty of room for growth.

There are many rhododendrons (some scented) that can be grown in containers that flower in late spring and early summer. Again, they need acid soil. Suitable small varieties include 'Blue Diamond', violet-blue; *R. calostratum*, rose-pink; 'Cilpinense', pale pink; 'Doc', rose-pink; 'Greeting', orange-red; *R. kiusianum*, pink to purple; 'Moerheim', violet-blue; *R. sargentianum*, lemon-yellow; 'Snow Lady', pure white; and 'Vida Brown', rose-pink.

Other good shrubs for the spring include *Spiraea japonica* 'Goldflame', bronze-red young leaves, and some of the viburnums. Eventually most viburnums grow too large for a normal container garden, but the lovely *V. plicatum* 'Mariesii' does not gallop away, and *V. p.* 'Rowallene' is reasonably compact with leaves that turn dark red before they fall in the autumn.

Early-flowering clematis

The most popular spring-flowering climber is the clematis. *C. armandii* is evergreen with heavily scented white flowers in early spring, but it is not totally hardy and is extremely vigorous. You do need plenty of room to grow it. A better choice for the container gardener would be one of the *alpina* and *macropetala* varieties that flower from mid-spring into early summer. They are totally hardy, although they will not tolerate wet soil. They are quite small, usually only reaching 3m/10ft in height and are exactly right for growing in containers. They should be pruned lightly when flowering is over in midsummer, and only cut back hard if they have outgrown their allotted space. Alpinas have single bell-shaped flowers and include 'Frances Rivis', lantern-like mid-blue flowers; 'Rosy Pagoda', pale

▶ *Small fruit trees can produce surprisingly good crops when grown in containers. They should be fan-trained, espaliered or minarette.*

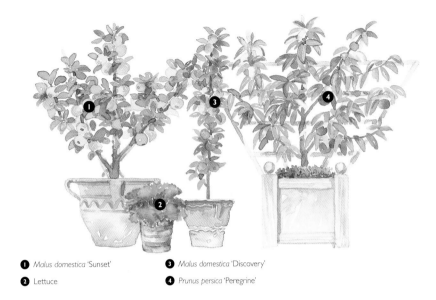

1 *Malus domestica* 'Sunset'
2 Lettuce
3 *Malus domestica* 'Discovery'
4 *Prunus persica* 'Peregrine'

spring is one of the real bonuses. The earliest fruit trees to flower are the peach and apricots, followed by pears, then apples. Peach and apricot flower on bare branches early in spring before the leaves appear. The flowers are single, pink or red, and it is essential to protect them whenever any late frost threatens. Pears have clusters of white flowers just as the trees are starting to come into leaf. The blossom arrives earlier than on the apple trees and covers the trees with white flowers. Plums and gages have white blossom about the same time as the pear trees, that also emerges just as the trees are starting to come into leaf. It is not so spectacular as pear blossom.

Apples have probably the loveliest blossom of all, and it is something that no keen gardener should be without. The pink-tinged white flowers open from pink buds later in the spring. Some of the crab apple varieties have blossom in many colours, which range from pure white to deep rose-pink.

Spring-flowering perennials

There are not all that many perennials that flower in spring, and the container gardener with only a small amount of space is, perhaps, better to concentrate

on spring bulbs, which are reliable and always lovely to look at. If you have got room though, probably the best spring perennial is lungwort, *Pulmonaria*. There are different kinds (many with spotted leaves), which look a bit like the inside

of the lung, hence their name. They are one of the sights of spring and have erect sprays of pink, white, red, blue and purple flowers that last for several weeks. They prefer shade and will spread quite freely, providing good cover.

▶ *Apple blossom is probably the loveliest of all with its pink-edged petals. You need at least two varieties of apple trees for pollination.*

container gardening in summer

Summertime is when gardens look at their best. The trees are in new leaf and many plants are in flower. The favourite garden flowers for containers in summer are the summer annuals. But for any gardener who wants to be different there is a multitude of choices, some unusual, some well known.

Summer-flowering bulbs

When people think of bulbs they inevitably think of spring bulbs but there are many that flower in summer. They should not be ignored because they are quite easy to grow, and many are ideal in containers. They include Peruvian lilies, *Alstroemeria* Ligtu Hybrids, in a multitude of pastel shades in late summer; *Galtonia candicans* and *G. viridiflora*, with white lily-like flowers that need some protection in hard winters; *Gladiolus*, extremely popular corms, available in

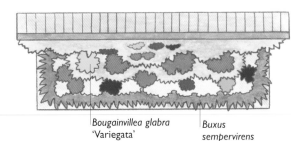

Bougainvillea glabra 'Variegata'   Buxus sempervirens

◀ *Climbers and shrubs in shades of red, pink and purple can be grouped in a sunny sheltered position. Add some white flowers to highlight the colours.*

many sizes and colours; Jacobean lily, *Sprekelia formosissima*, with beautiful red flowers in early summer, but needing a warm south wall and winter protection; and the peacock flower, *Tigridia pavonia*, a most exotic-looking flower rather like an orchid with an inner spotted face – Choice Mixture has flowers from yellow through orange to red.

Lilies

Lilies are a huge genus with over 100 species and countless hybrids. There are six divisions. They need to be staked in advance so that the stems of the plants

◀ *Lilium 'Sun Ray' is quite a small lily with bright yellow flowers, lightly dotted with brown. Although a good container plant, it is not scented.*

are held upright as they grow. Otherwise they will flop over. Grown in a container the bulbs should be planted in deep pots in fertile compost made up with equal parts of loam, peat substitute and leaf mould, and the addition of some well-rotted manure or slow-release fertiliser. Cover the bulbs with at least 7.5cm/3in of compost. Among the best are the Asiatic Mixed hybrids, smaller than the trumpet lilies, but very suitable for a large container, and the showy trumpet lilies. The latter includes *L. speciosum* var. *rubrum* with pink flowers and red spots, regal lily, *L. regale*, with wonderfully scented white inner flowers, striped purple-violet on the outside, and *L. r.* var. *album* with almost pure white flowers. There are also yellow or orange ones.

planting summer bulbs

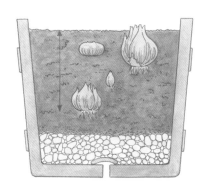

1 It is easiest to plant the bulbs and fill the container at the same time. As a general rule, plant bulbs deeply, at least 2½ times the height of the bulb.

2 In a raised bed or open ground a bulb planter is a helpful tool. Most have various depths marked on the sides and are hinged so you can remove the soil.

3 Some bulbs have to be planted just below or on the surface. These include amaryllis and hyacinths grown in containers for flowering indoors.

Summer-flowering shrubs and climbers

The temptation to rely on annuals entirely in the summer garden should be resisted. All gardens look better for varied planting, with shrubs and climbers adding colour at different height levels.

Climbers that flower in summer include the coral plant, *Berberidopsis corallina*, that needs shade, acid soil and protection in hard winters. It is evergreen and carries dark red ball-like flowers on long stalks that hang down the length of the branches. *Bougainvillea glabra* is a strong-growing evergreen climber that can be grown in containers, provided

that it is pruned hard to keep it within bounds. It is suitable for gardens free of winter frost. The flowers are normally brilliant shades of purple and red.

Summer is also a good time for the large-flowered clematis. They can be

trained along a trellis and up a wall. The most attractive are 'Comtesse de Bouchaud', pink; 'Jackmanii Superba', violet; 'Henryi', creamy white; 'Marie Boisselot', white; 'Lasurstern', lavender-blue; and 'Nelly Moser', pinkish-mauve.

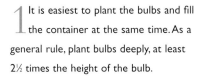

▶ *Bougainvillea grows quite happily in containers provided it is kept free from frost and placed in a warm sunny position.*

Like the climbing hydrangea which it resembles, *Schizophragma hydrangeoides* clings by aerial roots. It has fragrant, tiny white flowers in summer that are surrounded by creamy white bracts. The effect is quite striking and it looks good against a coloured plain background. It needs a bit of space and in a container garden is most suited to a permanent bed against a wall. Plant 60cm/2ft away from the bricks, and tie the plant to a support until it becomes established.

The Confederate jasmine, *Trachelospermum jasminoides*, is another evergreen climber that grows in partial shade, and does best in neutral to slightly acid soil. The leaves turn bronze-red in winter. It is not fully hardy and does not tolerate strong winds. The flowers appear in mid to late summer and are pure white with five flat petals, rather like a miniature catherine wheel.

Flame creeper, *Tropaeolum speciosum*, is another unusual climber but it can be maddeningly difficult to get established, and may need shelter in hard winters. It requires a deep container, neutral to acid soil, and the roots need to be cool at all times but with the flowers in the sun. Once established it will scramble up other plants or a trellis and has trails of brilliant, bright red flowers from midsummer onwards. It looks at its best when it is allowed to peep out prettily through a wall shrub.

◀ *Summer jasmine is an attractive climber, semi-evergreen in mild climates, with scented white flowers in summer. It needs controlling.*

Flowering shrubs for the summer garden

There are a number that can be considered. Flowering maple, *Abutilon*, is frequently trained against a south-facing wall because it needs sun and warmth. 'Boule de Neige' is evergreen with bell-shaped white flowers from spring through the summer, *A.* x *suntense* is deciduous with violet-blue flowers, 'Gorer's White' has white flowers, and *A. vitifolium* 'Veronica Tennant' has pink to mauve flowers.

Pineapple broom, *Cytisus battandieri*, is another shrub usually grown against a south-facing wall because it needs sun and warmth. In late summer it carries large clusters of fragrant bright yellow flowers that look a bit like miniature pineapples and have a pineapple scent. *Deutzia* is one of the more unusual shrubs that carries fragrant white to pink flowers in clusters from the middle of spring through to midsummer. Two of the best kinds are *D.* x *elegantissima* 'Rosealind' with pink flowers and the pink *D.* 'Mont Rose' with violet-streaked petals. Both can be accommodated in a medium-sized container.

The flannel bush, *Fremontodendron* 'California Glory', is another evergreen wall shrub that should be trained against a south-facing wall. It will usually tolerate occasional low temperatures. It has beautiful large yellow flowers throughout the summer from late spring onwards. *Hebe* is a large genus of evergreen shrubs, many of which have spikes of blue, white, pink and lilac

▶ Hostas come in a wide variety of leaf colours, yellow to smoky grey, with pale white to violet flowers held on spikes in summer.

flowers, although there is a great variety of flower colour and form. Some make large shrubs, and other species, such as *H. cupressoides* 'Boughton Dome', are suitable for growing in alpine gardens. Two smallish popular shrubs suitable for containers are *H.* 'Bowles Hybrid' that has lavender-blue flowers and *H. pinguifolia* 'Pagei', pure white.

Summer perennials There is a great tendency to ignore perennials in a summer container garden. This should be resisted as they can be very attractive and are good for filling bare spaces. They are best used in two ways. If you have the room you can make a careful plan to create a small herbaceous border using specially bred miniature varieties of common herbaceous flowering plants, such as lupins, hollyhocks and delphiniums; some of the smaller varieties of hardy geraniums, phlox, penstemons, pinks or scabious are also suitable for such a plan.

The second approach that can be extremely effective, and is better where room is constricted, is to choose some of your favourite perennials and plant them in individual containers where they can be grouped with other plants. Hostas are ideal, as are some of the lower-growing plants, such as the pincushion flower, *Scabiosa caucasica*, or the blue balloon flower, *Platycodon grandiflora* 'Mariesii'.

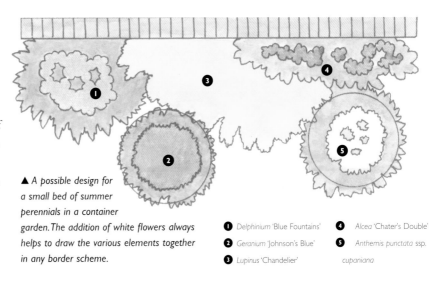

▲ A possible design for a small bed of summer perennials in a container garden. The addition of white flowers always helps to draw the various elements together in any border scheme.

❶ *Delphinium* 'Blue Fountains'

❷ *Geranium* 'Johnson's Blue'

❸ *Lupinus* 'Chandelier'

❹ *Alcea* 'Chater's Double'

❺ *Anthemis punctata* ssp. *cupaniana*

container gardening in autumn

For many people, autumn is the loveliest time of the year. The season is over, the crops have ripened, the leaves on the trees turn yellow and gold and then fall to the ground, slowly at first but with increasing speed as the first frosts or autumn gales shorten their lives.

The importance of autumn colour

Autumn colour does not last for ever and depends very much on the weather, rain or sun, frost or warm wet winds, but it is something to be treasured and every garden, however big or small, should contain some plants that look their best at this time of year. Among the most popular are the Japanese maples, varieties of *Acer palmatum*, that are generally slow growing, making mounded shrubs, although eventually they become too big for the average container. They have mid-green leaves in the summer, but in the autumn these change to varied shades of orange, yellow, red and gold.

The varieties 'Burgundy Lace', 'Butterfly', 'Garnet' and 'Red Pygmy' are all good and widely available. They prefer sun or partial shade and slightly acid soil.

Another shrub that does not grow too quickly and that provides sensational autumn colour is *Fothergilla major*. It prefers neutral to acid soil and has small, white, bottlebrush flowers in late spring and early summer. In the autumn the leaves turn from yellow through orange to red, blue and black before falling. They stand out like the brightest flower in the garden in high summer.

Autumn berries

Many of the best berries are much appreciated by birds and squirrels, and do not remain long on the trees. Rowan berries, for example, hardly last any time at all. Small crab apples are not so popular and can be grown for their bright red and yellow fruit, as well as the lovely apple blossom in spring. They are

◀ *The brilliant red berries and bronze leaves of cotoneaster 'Cornubia' are spectacular in autumn. It is a large shrub and needs space.*

▶ 'Lucifer' is a dwarf canna lily that stays in flower from midsummer until autumn. They need a warm site and water in dry spells.

suitable trees for a container garden, provided there is room to grow them as pyramids – 'John Downie' has red fruit, and 'Golden Hornet' bright yellow. Both have the advantage of being self-fertile, and if they are grafted on to a dwarfing rootstock they will not grow too large.

Snowberry, *Symphoricarpos* × *doorenbosii*, is another possibility. Grow it on its own in a container because it has a suckering habit and spreads too freely if unconfined. The autumn berries are slightly poisonous to humans and are not appreciated by birds so they may remain on the bushes for many months during the winter. The best-known varieties are 'White Hedge' with clusters of white berries, and 'Mother of Pearl' with pinkish berries.

Firethorn, *Pyracantha*, is well-known for its clusters of berries, as is hawthorn,

Crataegus. Hawthorns are too large for a container garden, but smaller shrubs include shallon, *Gaultheria shallon*, and varieties of *G. mucronata*. Like the

snowberry, they are suckering shrubs and need to be confined in a single container. They were formerly known as *pernettya* and must be grown in acid soil. They have prominent round berries in colours ranging from white to magenta, depending on the variety grown.

The other excellent shrub for autumn and winter colour is *Skimmia japonica*. The many forms have bright red berries and small varieties fit well into window boxes where they brighten the winter months. The only drawback if you wish to grow them as permanent shrubs in a container garden, is that both male and female plants are necessary if they are to flower and bear fruit.

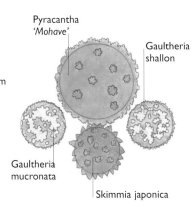

Nerine bowderii

Colchicum autumnale C. byzantinum

Cyclamen hederifolium

Cyclamen hederifolium

Colchicum autumnale C. byzantinum

▲ Autumn bulbs are at their best either growing in drifts in grassland or, in the case of nerines, given the shelter of a warm wall.

Pyracantha 'Mohave'

Gaultheria shallon

Gaultheria mucronata

Skimmia japonica

▲ Always consider whether any shrub in the garden has coloured berries in autumn. This is a bonus for birds as well as gardeners.

The most spectacular climber of the autumn is Virginia creeper. The best one to grow is Boston ivy, *Parthenocissus tricuspidata* and its varieties. The true Virginia creeper is *P. quinquefolia*, that used to be known by the charming Latin name of *Vitis inconstans*; this provides a brief show of autumn glory before the leaves fall. A number of the oriental vines also provide brilliant colour, *Vitis coignetiae* and *V. vinifera* 'Purpurea' are the two most commonly grown. Golden hop, *Humulus lupulus* 'Aureus', is another climber whose leaves turn golden yellow in the autumn. One climber that gives autumn flowers and colour is the small-flowered *Clematis tangutica* and its varieties that have nodding yellow flowers, followed by attractive silver seedheads.

Autumn bulbs

Autumn bulbs are dominated by the autumn crocus, *Colchicum*, that flowers from late summer through the autumn into winter, depending on the species grown. The most common is meadow saffron, *C. autumnale*, that has pink flowers. It has a number of varieties, 'Alboplenum' is white and 'Pleniflorum' has rounded pink flowers. Other popular species are *C. byzantinum*, with pinkish-lilac flowers, and *C. speciosum* with flowers of a deeper pink. The variety *C. s.* 'Album' has pure white flowers shaped like wine goblets. The flowers of autumn crocuses emerge before the leaves giving them their other common name, Naked Ladies. A number will naturalise in the wild but all can be grown in containers. Plant them in a deep container in well-drained compost in late summer.

There are two other notable autumn-flowering bulbs or corms that grow well in containers. Guernsey lily, *Nerine bowdenii*, is one. It prefers to be pot-bound and needs a warm sunny position. It produces sprays of pink flowers that last for several weeks. The second is the autumn cyclamen, varieties of *C. hederifolium*, that you may still find sold under its former name of

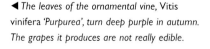
◀ *The leaves of the ornamental vine,* Vitis vinifera 'Purpurea', *turn deep purple in autumn. The grapes it produces are not really edible.*

▶ *Smaller dahlias can be grown in small spaces in containers. Some of the dwarf mixtures available that only grow to 60cm/2ft are ideal.*

C. neapolitanum. They have charming little flowers in shades of pink to white held aloft on stalks. They are also suitable plants for an alpine garden.

Dahlias

Dahlias are the autumn flower. No other plant is so easy to cultivate or provides such spectacular blooms, and you have a choice of over 20,000 varieties. Dahlias are divided into 11 groups depending on the shape of their flowerheads. These vary from single through pompom to orchid and peony. Some are enormous with flowerheads over 25cm/10in in diameter, but many are much neater with flowerheads under 10cm/4in across. The colours range from pink, red, yellow through orange and white. Anyone who wants to cultivate dahlias should consult a specialist catalogue to choose dahlias of the type, size and colour that will suit

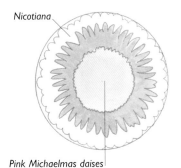

Nicotiana

Pink Michaelmas daises

▲ *Plant a container with* Aster novae-belgii *'Apple Blossom' and surround it with tobacco plants, such as* Nicotiana *'Domino White'.*

their garden. Plant the tubers in mid to late spring when all danger of frost has passed. The plants need to be staked, and this is best done at planting to avoid damaging the tubers. Plant them at least 10cm/4in deep in fertile compost, and add a phosphate-based fertiliser (bonemeal is the easiest). Protect the young shoots from slugs.

Autumn-flowering perennials

The most popular autumn-flowering perennials are Michaelmas daisies, *Aster novi-belgii*, and their twin the New England aster, *A. novae-angliae*; both come into bloom when almost all other

flowers have finished flowering. They carry clumps of daisy-like flowers in varying colours from blue and lilac, to pink and white, and a number have the typical yellow centres of the daisy family. They are quite tall plants and generally reach about 1.2m/4ft and do require staking at this height. They are not particularly suitable for a small container garden. *A. n-b.* 'Apple Blossom' is pure pink and 'Marie Ballard' a delicate light blue. Another good autumn perennial is *Ceratostigma willmottianum*. This has leaves that turn red in the autumn, and attractive pale blue flowers shaped like those of the periwinkle.

61

plant directory

The range of plants for containers is wide, from summer-flowering bedding plants to bulbs, hardy herbaceous perennials and shrubs. This comprehensive parade of plants will guide you through the often perplexing but invariably exciting job of choosing plants. Each plant is thoroughly described, with information about its size and shape and the colour of its flowers and leaves. Some plants have preferences about composts and this, too, is given in this extensive directory of plants.

Trees

FRUIT TREES
Malus domestica
Apple
Height 1.8m/6ft

Spread 1.8m/6ft

These are grown most successfully in
containers as cordons or espaliers trained
against a wall, and are a popular choice on
roof gardens, where they can be used to
divide up the space. Grafted on an M9
dwarfing rootstock, they occupy 1.8m/6ft
and 3m/10ft of wall space respectively,
both 1. 8m/6ft high, so make sure this
amount of space is available. Minarette
trees, single standards, can be grown as
freestanding trees in containers and reach
1.8–2.4m/6–8ft. Most apples need a
pollinator, so two varieties need to be
grown, unless a neighbouring garden has
apple trees. Check with the nursery before
buying as some varieties will not pollinate
others. Favourite apples include:
'Discovery'; 'Fiesta', 'Queen Cox' (eating);
'Arthur Turner'; 'Lord Derby' (cooking).

Pyrus communis
Pear
Height 1.8m/6ft

Spread 1.8m/6ft

Pears are grown in the same way as apples
but they are trickier for the blossom
flowers earlier in the year and is thus more
liable to damage by late frosts. They prefer
a south- or southwest-facing wall. In a
container garden they should be grafted on
Quince C or Quince A rootstock. Quince
C is the most dwarfing. As with apples you
need to grow two compatible varieties at
the same time for they are not reliably self-
fertile. Check with the nursery when
buying. Favourite pears include:
'Concorde'; 'Conference'; 'Doyenne du
Comice'; 'Williams Bon Chrétien'.

Prunus domestica
Plum
Height 1.8.m/6ft

Spread 3.7m/12ft fan-trained

In a container garden plums should be
grafted on to Pixy rootstock and trained as
a fan. Fan-training is more difficult than

training an espalier, and a good pruning
manual will provide instructions.
Minarettes are also available. It is best
in limited space to grow one of the self-
fertile varieties, such as, 'Czar', 'Early
Transparent Gage', 'Merryweather
Damson' (if you like damsons), 'Opal' or
the old favourite 'Victoria'. This last one
will grow quite well in a certain amount
of shade.

ORNAMENTAL TREES
Acer palmatum var. *dissectum*
Japanese maple
Height 1.8m/6ft

Spread 3m/10ft (after some years)

Japanese maples are ideal container plants.
They create an Oriental feel in a small
garden. They hug the ground and the
long, feathery, deeply divided leaves hang
down most attractively. Their chief glory is
the wonderful shades of red, yellow and
purple that the leaves turn in autumn. If
you cannot find *A. c.* var. *dissectum*, choose
one of the slow-growing varieties, such as,
A. p. Dissectum Atropurpureum Group.

Pyrus communis 'Conference'

Prunus domestica

Acer palmatum var. *dissectum*

Ilex aquifolium

green leaves and white scented flowers in spring followed by orange or yellow fruit. Lemon trees have pale green leaves and exceptionally fragrant flowers followed by lemons. The variety 'Meyer' is the one most usually grown for it has a more compact habit than the species. Both of these small trees make an excellent focal point in a container garden in the summer, especially if planted in a grand terracotta urn.

Ilex aquifolium
Holly
Height 3m/10ft
Spread 2m/6ft

Hollies should be grown in containers more often than they are for they grow very slowly and have good evergreen foliage and lovely red berries in the winter that can be cut for Christmas decoration. They can also be clipped and trained as low-growing hedges. The male variety 'Silver Queen' has white-edged leaves and the female 'J. C. van Tol' has dark green leaves. Both male and female plants are needed to produce berries.

Camellia × williamsii 'Donation'
Camellia
Height 5m/16ft
Spread 2.5m/8ft

Camellias can either be classified as a small tree or shrub. Eventually, growing in the wild under favourable conditions, they reach considerable proportions. But they are slow-growing and tolerant of pruning, so can be confined satisfactorily in containers for many years. They make ideal formal small trees with their neat pointed evergreen leaves and perfect flowers in early spring. They need both shade and acid soil to flourish. There are many varieties. Most camellias are pink, white or red. *C.* 'Donation' is widely grown in container gardens and has pink semi-double blooms. It prefers deep shade.

× Citrofortunella microcarpa/
Citrus limon
Calamondin orange/lemon tree, citrus tree
Height and spread 45–60cm/18–24in

Citrus trees grown indoors as pot plants in temperate climates are good small decorative trees to put out on patios in the summer, provided these are sheltered and sunny. The calamondin orange has dark

Camellia 'Leonard Hessel'

Laurus nobilis
Bay tree, sweet bay
Height 12m/40ft

Spread 9m/30ft

Growing in the wild in good conditions the evergreen bay tree can become quite large. However it is justifiably one of the most popular trees for all container gardeners for it does not resent being confined in a pot, it grows pretty slowly, and it can be clipped to shape to make balls, mopheads and cones. Grown and trained as a standard it is a dignified tree that is welcome in many small gardens and on patios and balconies. The leaves are dark green and pointed and are used to flavour marinades and sauces in the kitchen. Bay trees have small white, insignificant flowers in spring, followed by tiny black fruits.

Olea europaea
Olive
Height and spread: 6m/20ft or more

The slow-growing olive from the Mediterranean is increasingly grown in containers in temperate climates. Winters are getting milder and small trees can always be given some shelter in very hard weather. Olives are evergreen with pointed leaves, grey-green above and silvery-grey beneath. The trees form a rounded head. They need a good fertile compost and feeding with liquid fertiliser every month in the growing season. The small white flowers are fragrant and the fruit starts green, turning black as it ripens.

Conifers
Conifers are one of the mainstays of the container and alpine garden. The varieties described are all slow growing and have different-coloured foliage. Grouped together they provide contrast of shape and colour.

Cedrus deodara 'Feelin' Blue'
Deodar cedar
Height 30cm/12in

Spread 90cm/3ft

Most cedars are large trees that require a good deal of room but a number of new varieties have been developed as dwarf forms that can be grown in container gardens and in alpine beds where space is limited. This deodar cedar has a weeping habit with attractive blue-green leaves and branches that hang down. Like all cedars it prefers well-drained moist soil and full sun. Other small cedars include *C. deodara* 'Golden Horizon', slightly larger, the leaves will be darker and bluer if grown in shade; and *C. d.* 'Aurea', golden foliage.

Chamaecyparis lawsoniana 'Barry's Silver'
False cypress
Height 1.5m/5ft

Spread 75cm/30in

There are a number of false cypresses with varying foliage colours. 'Barry's Silver' is a comparatively recent introduction that originated in New Zealand. It is quite slow growing and in the summer the tips of the new leaves appear silvery white, changing to green. It has an upright habit. It is best planted in a sheltered position in full sun where the soil does not dry out. Other varieties include 'Little Spire' blue-green, and 'Stardust', yellow.

Laurus nobilis

Juniperus communis 'Compressa'

Buxus sempervirens

Juniperus communis 'Compressa'
Common juniper

Height 30cm/12in

Spread 9cm/4in

Probably the most popular conifer for the small garden, *J. c.* 'Compressa' makes a slender compact column, bright green with silver-backed foliage. It is extremely slow growing and is most unlikely to outgrow its allotted station in the garden. It is suitable for planting in window boxes if needs be to add some vertical interest, and looks well in an alpine garden. *J. c.* 'Depressa Aurea' is another good small juniper with golden yellow leaves in summer, turning bronze-green in winter. It will eventually reach 30cm–1. 5m/2–5ft.

Picea glauca 'Alberta Blue'
White spruce

Height and spread: 45–60cm/18–24in

A lovely conical dwarf conifer with intense silvery-blue new shoots in early summer that gradually darken as summer progresses. This is another dwarf conifer that looks ideal in alpine gardens and all forms of container. It prefers sun or light shade and well-drained soil. *P. abies* 'Ohlendorffii' is another slow-growing spruce suitable for the container garden that has dark green foliage, and is definitely ball-shaped. It might eventually reach 3m/10ft in height.

Thuja orientalis 'Raffles'
Red cedar

Height 30–45cm/12–18in

Spread 30cm/12in

One of the bonuses in growing red cedars is the changing colours of the foliage throughout the year. The variety 'Raffles' has yellowish-green leaves in spring but these turn to reddish-bronze as the cold winds of autumn come at the end of the year. It is small and slow-growing with a conical habit and very suitable for a container of conifers. The plant is poisonous and the leaves are harmful if eaten.

Shrubs

Buxus sempervirens
Common box

Height (grown as a tree): 5m/16ft

Spread 5m/16ft

Box is actually a tree, but it is virtually always grown as a small shrub, used for formal edging and topiary in many gardens throughout the world. Box is an essential ingredient in all knot gardens and a neat, clipped low-growing box hedge conveys an instant impression of professional competence. In containers box is very often found trained into various topiary shapes, for the small leaves lend themselves to clipping to shape. A number of good

Fatsia japonica

varieties have been developed: 'Aureovariegata' has variegated gold-splashed leaves; 'Elegantissima' is very dense; and 'Suffruticosa' is compact and slow growing.

Exochorda × *macrantha* 'The Bride'
Pearl bush

Height 1.2m/4ft

Spread 1.5m/5ft

This is a slow-growing shrub very suitable for any container or small garden. It flowers in late spring or early summer and flourishes in sun or partial shade. In flower it is one of the most beautiful shrubs in the garden with cascades of pure white flowers hanging down the pendent branches. It deserves to be better known. The flowers are born on the previous year's growth and it is better if left unpruned. Exochordas flourish in most garden soils but do best in neutral soil. Some species dislike lime.

Fatsia japonica
Japanese aralia

Height and spread: 1.5m/5ft

This is an architectural shrub grown entirely for its shape and large sculptural evergreen leaves. It does have small clumps of white flowers in late summer that appear on long stalks, which look a bit like a space station from a sci-fi movie, but they are very insignificant, as are the black berries that follow them. The plants are not fully hardy but they tolerate shade and pollution and make excellent container plants in a town garden for their large leaves are very striking. There are a number of varieties.

× *Halimiocistus wintonensis*

Height 60cm/2ft

Spread 90cm/3ft

Another small shrub that deserves to be a great deal better known than it is, and it is a good addition to any container garden. The genus is a cross between *Cistus* and *Halimium*, the rock roses, and has many of the qualities of the parents. All are excellent shrubs to include in an open sunny position and look well with other rock roses in an alpine garden. The shrubs are evergreen with grey-green leaves and the flowers are a beautiful white saucer shape with yellow stamens in the centre surrounded by a dark maroon band.

Hebe 'Rosie'
Hebe

Height 30cm/1ft

Spread 60cm/2ft

Hebes are a large genus with over 100 species of evergreen shrubs of varying sizes, ranging from 2.5m/8ft to dwarf species suitable for rock and scree gardens. They vary in hardiness. They are grown for their conical spikes of flowers, often blue, white or purple, that emerge in midsummer and last for a long time. 'Rosie' is a comparatively new, dwarf variety, very suitable for containers and alpine gardens that has lovely darkish-pink flowers that last for several months. It is very hardy.

Hydrangea macrophylla
Common hydrangea

Height 1.2m/5ft

Spread 1.8m/6ft

Hydrangeas make good container plants and create an instant and colourful effect in any garden. They should be planted on their own. The most striking is the hortensia division of *H. macrophylla*. These shrubs carry large heads of flowers, pink, white, blue and lilac, depending on the variety grown and the acidity of the soil. 'Générale Vicomtesse de Vibraye' is one of the best to grow. It makes a good container plant and can also be raised as an indoor plant when young. The flowers are either pale blue, if grown in acid soil, or varying shades of pink.

Kolkwitzia amabilis 'Pink Cloud'
Beauty bush

Height 3m/10ft

Spread 4m/13ft

This is another shrub that is seldom grown and deserves to be better known and used in all gardens, not just the container garden. In fact, it should be confined to its own container for it has a suckering habit. It is fairly slow growing and takes a long time to reach its full size. It needs fertile soil and prefers sun or partial shade. The glory of the shrub is the cascades of pink flowers that appear in late spring and hang down on the branches. The variety is preferred to the species plant as the flowers are a deeper pink. It is deciduous and the young leaves may become damaged by late frosts, so it may need some protection.

Lavandula angustifolia 'Hidcote'
Lavender

Height and spread 45cm-90cm/18in-3ft

Lavender is one of the very best shrubs to grow in a container garden, provided that it has a warm and sunny position, for it originally comes from the Mediterranean and like all shrubs from that region prefers sun and warmth. The leaves and flowers are both wonderfully fragrant, and it is good used as a dried flower to stuff scented pillows. The variety 'Hidcote' has dark purple flowers and is commonly grown. 'Munstead' has deep blue-purple flowers and 'Loddon Pink' has pink flowers. The other main lavenders grown are *L.* × *intermedia*, English lavender, and *L. stoechas*, French lavender. Prune all lavenders hard in the spring to keep them in shape.

Hydrangea macrophylla

Pieris formosa

Pieris formosa var. *forrestii*
Pieris

Height 4m/13ft

Spread 3.5m/11ft

Don't be put off growing a pieris by the eventual size that it might attain. They grow quite slowly and only achieve their maximum dimensions in optimum conditions. They are lovely shrubs for a spring container garden as the young leaves appear bright red, changing to light green as summer progresses, and the white flowers emerge from dark pink buds. They must be grown in acid soil and partial shade and dislike cold winds in spring. Varieties of *P. formosa* are fairly upright, 'Wakehurst' is very popular, those of *P. japonica* are more rounded in form.

Spiraea japonica 'Goldflame'
Spiraea

Height 1.8m/6ft

Spread 1.5m/5ft

Spiraeas are deciduous shrubs and a number are very suitable for containers and small gardens, for they hug the ground

Lavandula angustifolia 'Hidcote'

Spiraea japonica 'Goldflame'

forming low clumps. *S. j.* 'Goldflame' is one of the commonest and is largely grown for its golden, bronze to red, young leaves that emerge in spring, turning green as the year progresses, and again to gold with the onset of autumn. It also has spires of deep pink flowers from midsummer onwards. It prefers full sun and most fertile soils.

Small roses

Small roses belong to one of three groups: miniature roses, the smallest, that usually only reach 30cm/12in in height; patio roses that reach 45cm/18in; and dwarf polyantha roses that may reach 60–90cm/2–3ft.

'Baby Darling'
Miniature rose

Height 25cm/10in

Spread 45cm/18in

An excellent miniature rose with masses of small orange-pink, slightly open flowers. As with all miniature roses this is a good flowering plant for a very small patio garden or even a window box: some gardeners grow them as flowering hedges around beds or containers. Few miniature roses have much scent but the varieties 'Little Flirt', orange-red flowers, and 'Yellow Doll', soft yellow flowers, are both slightly scented.

'Stars 'n' Stripes'
Miniature rose

Height 30cm/12in

Spread 60cm/24in

Miniature roses are attractive bushy plants
with tiny flowers. They are extremely
useful in a container garden where there is
little room, and can even be grown in
window boxes. In large gardens they can
be grown as a small hedge. 'Stars 'n' Stripes'
was developed on the west coast of
America and has white flowers, blotched
and striped with red, like a miniature of
the old rose *R. gallica* 'Versicolor'. Other
miniature roses include; 'Dresden Doll',
pale pink moss-like flowers, and 'Pour Toi',
creamy white flowers.

'Sweet Dream'
Patio rose

Height and spread 45cm/18in

This is one of the best patio roses for it has
a mass of dark green foliage and the
flowers are an apricot-peach colour held
upright like many petalled cups. It is slightly
fragrant. Patio roses are just a bit larger than

miniature roses and they repeat flower well.
'Anna Ford' has semi-double orange-red
flowers and 'Gentle Touch' has lovely pale
pink flowers, shaped like a small hybrid tea
rose and gently fragrant. It is a bit smaller
than the first two. If you prefer stronger
colours, 'Bianco' is white, 'Bright Smile',
yellow and 'Fairy Damsel', deep crimson.

'Katharina Zeimet'
Dwarf polyantha

Height and spread 30–90cm/1–3ft

There are two types of dwarf polyantha
roses: those whose flowers resemble
rambler roses, which are close-packed and
held in large sprays, and the roses whose
flowers are shaped like small miniature
hybrid tea roses. Both are appealing.
'Katharina Zeimet' is one of the best of the
rambler types with white, fragrant flowers;
pink-flowered roses of this type include
'Coral Cluster' and 'Nathalie Nypels'.
'Cécile Brünner', the 'Sweetheart Rose' is
the best known of the hybrid tea forms.
The flowers are blush pink; 'Perle d'Or' is
similar with apricot flowers.

Climbing roses

Climbing roses need to be differentiated
from ramblers. Climbers have larger flowers
and most repeat flowerings. Most modern
climbers repeat throughout the summer.
Ramblers are often very vigorous – too
vigorous, in fact, for any container garden,
however wonderful they look growing
through an old tree.

'Blairii Number Two'
Bourbon

Height 4.5m/15ft

Spread 1.8m/6ft

A Bourbon rose, a class of rose that mostly
dates from the latter part of the 19th
century, 'Blairii Number Two' has retained
its popularity as a climber for 150 years. It
has beautiful, pink many-petalled, fragrant
flowers, darker in the centre, that pale
towards the edges. It really only flowers
once in summer, although there is a small
second flowering. The young leaves are
reddish green when they emerge, changing
to mid-green as the summer progresses. It
is sometimes prone to attacks of mildew.

'Compassion'
Modern climber

Height 3m/10ft

Spread 2.5m/8ft

One of the very best and most popular of
the modern climbers, 'Compassion' has
large tea-shaped flowers, paleish pink on
the outside and apricot-yellow on the
inside. They are substantial blooms and
deliciously fragrant, giving the lie to
anyone who says that modern roses have
no perfume. It repeat flowers throughout

Rosa 'Sweet Dream'

Rosa 'Compassion'

the summer and has a strong bushy growth with dark green leaves. It looks its best when grown as a focal point on a southfacing wall where the blooms make the most impact.

'Constance Spry'
English rose
Height 3.5m/12ft
Spread 3.5m/12ft
This is one of the first English roses bred by David Austin. It can be grown as a shrub but makes an excellent climber when the lax shoots are given support and tied in to a frame The flowers are huge, clear pink, with the most pronounced myrrh fragrance. It makes a definite statement in any garden. Its only disadvantage is that unlike so many of the English roses it only flowers once, but those who grow it think that the advantages outweigh this.

'Copenhagen'
Modern climber
Height 2.5m/8ft
Spread 2.5m/8ft
This is another modern climber with flowers of superb fragrance. They are medium-sized, hybrid tea-shaped and deep scarlet. The rose will repeat flower throughout the summer and looks exceptional if it is grown in company with a large-flowered white clematis, such as 'James Mason'. Another modern climber with deep red flowers that can be grown as an alternative is 'Crimson Cascade'. This rose is similar in size but has larger flowers. It is extremely vigorous and disease resistant.

'Golden Showers'
Modern climber
Height 3m/10ft
Spread 3m/10ft
One of the very best and most amenable of all the climbing roses, 'Golden Showers' has double, clear yellow flowers that fade to a paler cream as they age. It repeat flowers throughout the summer and the flowers have a pleasing fragrance. Its main advantage is that it will flourish happily on a north wall, making it invaluable for any garden denied the benefit of walls with better aspects. 'Danse du Feu' is another climber that will grow against a north wall. This rose has orange-scarlet flowers.

'Climbing Iceberg'
Floribunda
Height 3m/10ft
Spread 2.5m/8ft
The climbing form of the ever-popular 'Iceberg' is an excellent rose to grow against a wall and forms an admirable background to all other plants. The foliage is light green and the white flowers,

Rosa 'Constance Spry'

sometimes tinged with pale pink, are held in delicate sprays. Its only disadvantage is that it has little or no scent. 'Iceberg' remains in flower longer than almost any other rose in the garden and it is not unusual to be able to gather sprays in midwinter, on Christmas Day.

'Maigold'
Climber
Height 3.5m/12ft
Spread 3m/10ft
Like 'Golden Showers', 'Maigold' has some supreme advantages over other climbing roses as it is one of the toughest roses around, and be grown almost anywhere. It has superb bronze-yellow, semi-double flowers, which are produced in abundance. The flowers are extremely fragrant. It has a mass of dark glossy leaves and is generally disease-free but, alas, it only flowers once during the summer. It is probably the best rose to grow in poor conditions against a north-facing wall and should be considered by anyone who wants to grow a climbing rose and can only offer these conditions.

Rosa 'Copenhagen'

'New Dawn'
Modern climber

Height 3m/10ft

Spread 2.5m/8ft

A deservedly popular climbing rose was one of the first modern climbers. It is very vigorous, has lovely, glossy, light- to mid-green leaves, and delicate silvery pink flowers with a slightly deeper colour in the centre. The flowers are born in clusters and repeat throughout the summer. They have a light delicate fragrance. 'New Dawn' is not prone to disease and tolerates a partially shaded site although it should not be planted against a north-facing wall.

'Paul's Lemon Pillar'
Hybrid tea

Height 6m/20ft

Spread 3m/10ft

The classic pillar rose that is found in many gardens growing up pergolas or old tree stumps. It can be grown in containers at the foot of an arch and trained over a pergola. The rose has large, creamy lemon, tea-shaped, fully double flowers with petals

Rosa 'New Dawn'

that curl back at the edges. The flowers are very fragrant. The leaves are dark green. It is a strong, hardy, vigorous rose that should be tied in to make a columnar shape.

'A Shropshire Lad'
English rose

Height 2.5m/8ft

Spread 1.8m/6ft

This is another English rose that makes an excellent climber planted against a warm wall. It is a rose well worth growing for the flowers are large, of the typical cupped-rosette form found on many English roses and deliciously fragrant. The colour is a beautiful peachy pink, fading slightly as the flowers age. Although it will grow best as a climber against a south wall, it can be planted in any position in the garden.

Climbers and wall plants

Abutilon × *suntense* 'Violetta'
Flowering maple, Indian mallow

Height 5m/16ft

Spread 3m/10ft

Some abutilons are evergreen, some deciduous, and none are fully hardy, but varieties of the deciduous *A.* × *suntense* are among the easiest to grow if they can be provided with a sheltered south-facing wall. They make excellent plants for containers. Flowers of the species are large and saucer-shaped. The variety 'Violetta' has intense violet flowers that appear in late spring. Any frost-damaged shoots should be cut back to sound wood in spring.

Clematis alpina 'Frances Rivis'
Clematis

Height 4m/13ft

Spread 1.8m/6ft

The alpina varieties of clematis are very suitable for growing in containers for they are relatively small in size and far less vigorous than montanas. They flower in spring. The flowers are single, and bell-shaped, like narrow pixies' caps with pointed petals. 'Frances Rivis' is the largest of the alpinas and has lovely dark blue flowers followed by fluffy seedheads. The alpinas are very hardy and will survive planted in the most unpromising positions, but they will not tolerate water-logged soil.

Clematis tangutica
Clematis

Height 4. 5m/15ft

Spread 1. 8m/6ft

One of the latest flowering of the clematis that brightens the autumn, *C. tangutica* carries funny, solitary, bright yellow flowers, bell-shaped but whose ends often appear as if they are crimped together.

Rosa 'Paul's Lemon Pillar'

They have striking seedheads that remain on the plant over the winter. The variety 'Helios' is shorter in growth and particularly suitable for a small container garden and there are a number of other hybrids. It is fully hardy.

Fremontodendron 'California Glory'
Flannel bush

Height 3m/10ft

Spread 3m/10ft

Fremontodendrons must be grown against a wall. They need tying in and are not considered particularly hardy although they will survive surprisingly cold winters given adequate protection. They are evergreen with rather sparse dark green leaves, up to 7.5cm/3in long. They are grown for the large deep buttercup-yellow flowers that appear in late spring and continue throughout the summer. The flowers are a shallow saucer shape. They prefer deep soil, so plant in a large container and see that there is good drainage. Cut back any frost-damaged shoots to good wood in spring.

Hydrangea petiolaris syn. *H. anomala* ssp. *petiolaris*

Clematis tangutica

Hedera helix 'Glacier'
Common ivy, English ivy

Height 1.8m/6ft or more

Spread 1.8m/6ft

Hedera helix, the common English ivy, has given rise to a large number of varieties. These can be grown against a wall to provide evergreen cover throughout the year, used as ground cover or grown indoors as a house plant. The variety 'Glacier' is excellent for all these purposes. It has dark grey-green leaves with variegated margins marked silver and cream. When grown outside, it needs a sunny position to show its best colour.

Hydrangea petiolaris syn. *H. anomala* ssp. *petiolaris*
Climbing hydrangea

Height 10m/33ft

Spread 10m/33ft

This is one of the best shrubs to cover a wall for it is not fussy over situation or aspect, and grows well in extremely shaded town gardens. It is a vigorous shrub but it can be cut back hard each spring. It clings to the wall by aerial roots and the bright green leaves turn yellow in the autumn before they fall. In the summer it is covered with clusters of white flowers surrounded by prominent sterile flowers.

Jasminum officinale
Common jasmine, summer jasmine

Height and spread 12m/40ft

This is another vigorous climber often found growing in containers that will quickly cover a wall or trellis with its long trailing dark green shoots. Jasmine needs a frame to wind itself around. The flowers are white and emerge in summer, lasting into the early autumn. They are very fragrant. It is best to prune jasmine after flowering is over, when it will often need to be cut back quite hard to keep it within its allotted space. It does not grow well in cold exposed sites.

Lapageria rosea
Chilean bellflower

Height and spread: 5m/16ft

A twining climber that will need support and protection in cold winters and will only flourish with the aid of a warm shady wall, as it comes from the forests of Chile and does not like full sun. It also needs acid soil. However if you can provide suitable

conditions it is a most attractive plant, evergreen with long dark green leaves, and long flowers, pink or rose-pink in colour, and shaped a bit like narrow trumpets. These first appear in midsummer and last until the autumn.

Pyracantha 'Orange Glow'
Firethorn

Height and spread: 3m/10ft

These are tough evergreen shrubs that can easily be trained against a wall and will grow in any situation from full sun to full shade. The less sun the plants get the fewer flowers and fruit they will bear. When grown against a wall they should be cut back hard in spring and trained to wires and then again in summer to remove shoots growing outwards and reveal the clusters of berries. They have white flowers in spring followed by orange, red, or yellow berries that last through the winter.

Solanum crispum 'Glasnevin'
Chilean potato vine

Height and spread: 6m/20ft

There are two members of the potato family that are popular climbers, *S. crispum* and *S. jasminoides*. Both are evergreen or semi-evergreen, and both are only partly hardy. The variety 'Glasnevin' is the one most popularly grown in temperate climates and has proved it can survive quite severe winters, given the protection of a warm wall. They are all scrambling climbers and the young shoots generally need to be tied in to a trellis or some other support. 'Glasnevin' has lovely purple-blue flowers that last from summer into the autumn.

Perennials

Container gardeners concentrate more on annuals and climbers than they do on perennials. Nevertheless there are a number that should be considered as permanent features in the garden.

Agapanthus Headbourne hybrids
African lily

Height 90cm/3ft
Spread 45cm/18in

In spite of their common name agapanthus are herbaceous perennials that are popular plants for containers where they flourish. They are grown largely for their dramatic clusters of flowers that emerge in late summer and resemble huge balls of bluebells held aloft on a large thick stalk. They like a sunny position and have thick roots that store water in dry periods. *Agapanthus* are not fully hardy and may need some protection in hard winters, but the Headbourne Hybrids, and a number of the named varieties, such as 'Blue Giant' and 'Alice Gloucester' are generally hardier than the species.

Jasminum officinale

Pyracantha 'Orange Glow'

Aponogeton distachyos
Cape pondweed, water hawthorn

Spread 1.2m/4ft

A rhizomatous perennial, the water hawthorn comes from South Africa, and has large deep green oval leaves that float on the surface of the water, like those of a water lily. The plants carry small white hawthorn-scented flowers in spring, and again in autumn, that are held aloft on forked flowering branches about 5cm/2in above the water. It prefers full sun but will tolerate partial shade. The water hawthorn is a good plant to grow to restrict the spread of algae in a pond or water garden.

Aquilegia vulgaris
Granny's bonnets, columbine

Height 90cm/3ft

Spread 45cm/18in

A favourite cottage garden perennial that flowers in late spring and early summer and is suitable for growing in any container, either on its own, or in company with other flowers. Granny's bonnets have dark

Solanum crispum 'Glasnevin'

blue-violet flowers, and a number of the varieties have flowers varying from white, through pale shades of blue, to pink and yellow. They are the most attractive flowers, rising on long stalks above pools of green leaves. They self-seed freely and when they are grown in a confined space need to be controlled ruthlessly.

Aster novi-belgii
Michaelmas daisies

Height 90–120cm/3–4ft

Spread 60–90cm/2–3ft

Michaelmas daisies are one of the most colourful plants to be found in the container garden, and they flower in the late summer and early autumn. They are usually found in varying shades of pink, violet, purple and white and most of them have the typical yellow centre of the daisy family. Among the most attractive are 'Marie Ballard', pale blue; 'Jenny', and 'Royal Ruby', deep pink; 'Lassie', pale pink and 'Kristina', white. They like well-drained soil and will flourish in partial shade. They require staking when grown in containers.

Aster novi-belgii

Dicentra formosa
Wild bleeding heart

Height 45cm/18in

Spread 60cm/2ft

D. spectabilis, bleeding heart or Dutchman's trousers, is a favourite spring border perennial. However it is probably too large for the average container garden and a better choice for a confined space is *D. formosa*, that spreads quite freely and has charming small purple flowers held up rather like branches of purple heather above silvery grey leaves. The variety 'Stuart Boothman' is very similar, slightly larger, and f. *alba* has white flowers and is less vigorous. They all flower in late spring and early summer and prefer some shade and neutral soil. Propagate by division.

Euphorbia amygdaloides
Wood spurge, milkweed

Height 75cm/30in

Spread 30cm/12in

There are over 2,000 species of euphorbia and they range in size from trees to tiny succulents. Probably the best-known garden euphorbia is *E. characias* ssp. *wulfenii*, which is a huge spectacular border plant. This, however, is not suitable for the average container garden. The wood spurge, *E. amygdaloides*, is much more suited as it is a small ground-covering plant that flourishes in shade. It has dark green leaves and green-yellow flowers that are held aloft on stalks. The variety 'Purpurea' has reddish-purple leaves and yellow flowers, and var. *robbiae*, 'Mrs Robb's bonnet', has much broader leaves. This variety may become invasive, so keep an eye on it.

Geranium farreri

room to accommodate it. It has great bushy flowerheads of bright yellow and does not really require staking. There are a number of other varieties including, 'Capenoch Star', single yellow flowerheads, and 'Soleil d'Or', double yellow flowerheads. They need to grow in full sun.

Helleborus orientalis
Hellebore, Lenten rose

Height 45cm/18in

Spread 45cm/18in

Lenten roses flower early in the year shortly after the Christmas rose, *H. niger*. The flowers are saucer-shaped and hang down from their stems. There are a number of colours and shades of mauve, pink, white and red are common. The flowers are attractively marked on the inside and remain on the plant for several weeks, at a time of the year when there is little else in flower. In mild climates the leaves are evergreen. There are many named varieties: Ashwood hybrids are popular. They need some shade and prefer to be sheltered from rain and wind if possible.

Geranium farreri
Cranesbill, hardy geranium

Height 10–15cm/4–6in

Spread 15cm/6in

Few garden plants provide as much pleasure to the gardener as the cranesbills. They flower throughout the summer and range in size from the spectacular *G. psilostemon*, to the tiny *G. farreri*, beloved by alpine gardeners. This small plant has flowers in an enchanting pale pink with conspicuous black anthers. Other favoured cranesbills that are suitable for a container garden include *G. wallichianum* 'Buxton's Variety', sky-blue with white veins and

dark anthers in the centre, and *G. clarkei* 'Kashmir White', which is white with deeper pink veins.

Helianthus × multiflorus
'Loddon Gold'
Perennial sunflower

Height 1.5m/5ft

Spread 90cm/3ft

Most sunflowers are grown as annuals and afford great amusement on the principle that 'I can grow a bigger one than you can.' The perennial sunflower, too, is quite a large plant but it can make a dynamic impact in a container garden if you have

Helleborus orientalis

Hosta 'Blue Moon'
Plantain lily

Height 10cm/4in

Spread 30cm/12in

Hostas grow better in containers than they do in borders where, in damp conditions, slugs devour them with an unbelievable relish. Slugs are not so prone to climb the sides of containers and the area is easier to control. Hostas are grown chiefly for their wonderful foliage, blue-grey, green, yellow-green and variegated white that, when grown together, can make such an impact in a shady garden where they flourish best. 'Blue Moon' is a small hosta with blue-grey foliage, 'Aureomarginata' has white-edged green leaves, and 'Gold Standard' has yellow leaves, edged with green.

Lobelia cardinalis
Cardinal flower

Height 90cm/3ft

Spread 30cm/1ft

The cardinal flower is a short-lived rhizomatous perennial with dark red stems and bright green, bronze-tinted leaves. It is grown for its brilliant scarlet flowers that emerge in late summer and early autumn. Few garden plants have such vivid colouring. The flowers can form the basis for a hot colour scheme in late summer. Cardinal flowers prefer deep, moist soil in full sun although they will tolerate partial shade. *L. erinus* varieties are low-growing trailing perennials usually grown as annuals.

Lupinus Gallery Hybrids
Lupins

Height 50cm/20in

Spread 20cm/8in

Many lupins, including the popular Russell Hybrids, are rather large for the average container garden, reaching 1.2m/4ft, but if you are seeking to create a cottage garden effect in a small space, then the smaller Gallery Hybrids, developed as a dwarf strain, are well worth considering. The colours are rather paler than the Russell Hybrids but there is a good choice of the traditional pale pink, yellow, blue, red, purple and lavender available. The flowers are more compact than in the larger varieties. Like all lupins they prefer a sunny position. Lulu Series and Dwarf Russell Mixed are two more small series.

Nymphaea 'Gonnère'
Water lily

Spread 90–120cm/3–4ft

Water lilies have to be chosen with care, and the ones that you can grow depend entirely on the depth of water and the size of your pool. 'Gonnère' is one of the most beautiful white water lilies, with many-petalled flowers, fragrant, with a clear yellow centre. It needs a pool about 90cm/3ft deep to flourish and its spread is less than many of the larger lilies. All water lilies grow best in full sun and they will not grow in running water, although some will tolerate very gentle movement.

Penstemon 'Andenken an
Friedrich Hahn'
Penstemon

Height 75cm/30in

Spread 60cm/24in

Penstemons are rather underrated as garden perennials, which is a pity. They make outstanding plants, evergreen or semi-evergreen, with long tubes of flowers from midsummer through into the autumn. They are easy to raise from cuttings taken in summer, or division in spring. They make excellent plants in a container garden if you do not want to include too many annuals. There are many excellent named varieties; three of the best known are: 'Andenken an Friedrich Hahn', deep red; 'Apple Blossom', a charming pink; and 'Maurice Gibbs', red with white centres.

Lobelia cardinalis

Lupinus

Phlox paniculata
Perennial phlox

Height 1.2m/4ft

Spread 60–90cm/2–3ft

Another glorious summer-flowering perennial that lasts in flower for weeks from the middle of summer into the autumn. There are many varieties in varying shades of pink, red, purple, lilac, blue and white. The glory of phloxes is their mop-headed flowers that look a bit like a colourful cloche hat on the top of the flower stalk. Among the most popular varieties are: 'Amethyst', violet; 'Eva Cullum', deep pink; 'Fujiyama', white; 'Le Mahdi', blue-purple; 'Mother of Pearl', white tinged with pink; and 'Prince of Orange', orange-red.

Primula vulgaris
Primrose

Height 20cm/8in

Spread 30cm/12in

Primulas are a large genus with over 400 species and thousands of varieties. In spite of this the common primrose, *P. vulgaris*,

has remained the firm favourite for many gardeners. The flowers are a delicate pale yellow, with a darker yellow centre. They are fragrant, and they have a charming modesty, as if apologising for rising above their green leaves. They are also extremely easy to grow and propagate through division when flowering is over. They prefer growing in some shade and will not flourish in hot, dry conditions.

Pulmonaria saccharata
Lungwort

Height 30cm/12in

Spread 60cm/24in

Pulmonarias are one of the loveliest sights in spring when the flowers emerge on stalks held above the blotched and spotted leaves that give the flower its common name. They are good plants to grow in a container, for they spread freely in open ground and if the container is raised the flowers can be inspected at eye level. Generally the flowers are blue or pink with some white varieties, and a number open pink and turn blue after some days. Blue and pink flowers are often present on the same flower stalk. There are a number of named varieties; Argentea Group has silvery leaves with red flowers turning violet, and 'Mrs Moon' has pink buds, opening to lilac-blue flowers.

Scabiosa caucasica 'Clive Greaves'
Scabious, pincushion flower

Height 60cm/2ft

Spread 60cm/2ft

Wild small scabious, *S. columbaria*, is a common and lovely wildflower, but the

genus is quite large and there are over 80 species. The cultivated varieties retain much of the charm of the parent and many have the lovely blue and lilac colouring, although various shades are available from purple to white. Scabious is a flower of the late summer when many others are over and should be planted to continue the flowering interest. 'Clive Greaves' has lavender-blue flowers, 'Bressingham White' has white, as does 'Mrs Willmott'.

Stachys byzantina
Lambs' ears, lambs' lugs

Height 45cm/18in

Spread 60cm/24in

Certainly one of the best-known grey foliage plants in the garden, Lambs' ears can be grown anywhere as a foil for the green foliage of so many garden plants. It makes a dense mat of silvery white, woolly, felted leaves topped in summer by purple lavender flowers held aloft on spikes. They prefer full sun and will tolerate most soils provided they are well drained. There are a number of varieties: 'Big Ears' has green

Phlox paniculata

Primula vulgaris

leaves with a grey bloom, and 'Silver Carpet' has silver leaves. This variety is grown as ground cover, for it does flower.

Annuals and bedding plants

These are the mainstay of the container gardener and different displays and colour schemes can be contrived from year to year, Some of the plants are perennials but they are normally grown as bedding plants.

Ageratum houstonianum
Floss flower

Height 15–30cm/6–12in

Spread 15–30cm/6–12in

Low-growing, half-hardy annuals that are native to Mexico. Blue, pink or white varieties can all be found although the most common colour is blue. The mounds of small flowers are held just above the foliage. There are a number of named varieties: those most commonly grown are the Hawaii Series, 'Red Sea' is purple-red, 'Blue Danube', a soft powder blue. Sow seed in spring at 16°C/60°F

Pulmonaria saccharata

Amaranthus caudatus
Love-lies-bleeding, tassel flower

Height 75cm/30in

Spread 45cm/18in

A hardy annual that has extraordinary crimson tassels that droop down. On some varieties the flower tassels are upright. It is rather larger than many annuals. Varieties of *A. tricolor* are bushy with vividly coloured leaves. Sow seeds in spring at 20°C/68°F.

Antirrhinum majus
Snapdragons

Height 30–45cm/12–18in

Spread 30cm/12in

These are half-hardy perennials that are normally grown as half-hardy annuals. They are a favourite flower of children who love popping the flowerheads open, hence the common name. The flowers come in all shades of brilliant colours, red, yellow, orange and white. There are a number of series: Rocket Series is the tallest, Sonnet Series flowers early and is intermediate in size, and both Tahiti Series and Magic Carpet Mixed are dwarfing.

Aubrieta × cultorum
Aubrieta

Height 5cm/2in

Spread 60cm/2ft

Aubrieta is a hardy perennial that can be propagated by seed sown indoors in early spring or outdoors in early summer. It forms trailing mats of blue flowers and is grown in cracks of walls. It needs to be clipped back after flowering. The flowers are nearly always purple-blue in colour, 'Hartswood Blue' and 'Joy' are popular.

Begonia
Begonias

Height 25cm/10in

Spread 30cm/12in

There are many different types of begonias but the ones usually grown in the summer garden are varieties of *B. tuberosa*, the tuberous begonias that have colourful large flowers, or *B. semperflorens*, which carry a mass of small flowers often with bronze foliage. Both should be treated as half-hardy annuals. There are an enormous variety of flower shapes and colours. Cocktail Mixed is a good *semperflorens* variety, the tuberous 'Royal Picotee' has huge yellow flowers.

Bellis perennis
Daisy

Height 15–20cm/6–8in

Spread 15cm/6in

Ornamental daisies are another hardy perennial usually treated as an annual. The flowers are held aloft on large pompoms and are red, pink or white in colour. They can be overwintered but most gardeners

Antirrhinum majus

replant them each year. Sow seed indoors at 10°C/50°F in early spring. The best known are the Pomponette, Roggli and Tasso Series, although there are many others that are available.

Brachyscome iberidifolia
Swan River daisy

Height 30cm/12in

Spread 30cm/12in

Popular small annuals that form clumps of flowers that appear as massed daisies, the colours are usually white, lilac-pink or purple. The Splendour Series is the one most commonly grown. Dwarf Bravo Mixed is a bit smaller and Summer Skies has flowers in attractively varied shades of blue, pink and white.

Calceolaria Herbeohybrida Group
Slipper flower, pouch flower, slipperwort

Height 25cm/10in

Spread 15cm/6in

These are half-hardy biennials normally grown as summer-flowering container

Calceolaria integrefolia

plants. They look like large bunches of small lozenges and are often a striking yellow or orange in colour. Sometimes the yellow varieties also have attractive orange drops in the centre. 'Bright Bikinis' has yellow, orange and red flowers, Anytime Series is compact and comes into flower very quickly. Sow seeds at 18°C/64°F in late summer or early spring.

Calendula officinalis
English marigold, pot marigold

Height 30–45cm/12–18in

Spread 30cm/12in

Extremely popular annuals that have been cultivated for many centuries. They are yellow and orange in colour and look rather like miniature chrysanthemums. They are hardy annuals so seed can be sown outside in spring or autumn where they are to flower. The Pacific Beauty Series is the most popular. *C. officinalis*, the traditional pot marigold, has single flowers.

Callistephus chinensis
China aster

Height 20–45cm/8–18in

Spread 20–45cm/8–18in

Half-hardy annuals that quickly make good bushy plants with flowers that are like miniature chrysanthemums in a multitude of colours: pink, yellow, red, mauve and white. Some of the more open varieties resemble Michaelmas daisies. There are many series. Among the best known are Ostrich Plume, Pompon Mixed, Milady Mixed and Colour Carpet. Sow seed at 15°C/60°F in early spring or outside later where the plants are to flower.

Campanula carpatica
Creeping bellflower

Height 30cm/12in

Spread 30–60cm/12–24in

There are many bellflowers, aptly named for their glorious bell-like flowers usually found in various shades of blue, purple and white. The creeping bellflowers are hardy perennials that make excellent edging plants for beds or pathways. They are extremely vigorous and may need to be controlled. The most popular varieties are 'Jewel', deep purple; 'Blue Gem'; blue, and 'Bressingham White'. In the spring, sow seed *in situ* or divide established plants.

Catananche caerulea
Cupid's dart, blue cupidone

Height 75cm/30in

Spread 30cm/12in

An attractive clump-forming, short-lived perennial with grey-green grass-like leaves in summer, that produces large numbers of single flowers on upright stalks, dark to pale blue, throughout the summer. It is sometimes grown as an annual. There are a

Calendula officinalis

number of named varieties. 'Bicolor' has
white petals with a purple centre, 'Major'
has lilac flowers with a dark centre, and
'Perry's White' has white flowers with a
creamy centre. The varieties need to be
raised by division or root cuttings for they
will not come true from seed.

Celosia argentea Plumosa Group
syn. *C. plumosa*
Prince of Wales's feathers
Height 20–50cm/8–20in

Spread 15–45cm/6–18in

There are two types of celosia: the
Plumosa Group that has upright plumes
and the Cristata Group that has rounded
tight flowerheads. The Plumosa Group are
those used in summer bedding schemes in
many parks and gardens. They appear in
very bright colours of yellow, pink, orange
and red and simply cannot be missed.
Varieties from the Century Series are the
most commonly grown, the Kimono Series
is smaller and more suited to a container
garden scheme. Sow seed at 18°C/64°F
from early spring onwards.

Campanula carpatica 'Blue Gem'

Chrysanthemum parthenium 'Aureum'

Centaurea cyanus
Cornflower, knapweed
Height 25–90cm/9–36in

Spread 15–25cm/6–10in

Cornflowers are hardy annuals available in
blue, claret, red or pink. However, the
traditional colour of the cornflower is deep
blue and many gardeners prefer to grow
this colour and no other. There are a
number of series, including the Standard
Tall Group and Baby Series, but individual
varieties are available, such as 'Blue
Diadem', 'Blue Ball' and 'Florence Blue'.
Sow seed *in situ* in spring or in autumn
the previous year.

Chrysanthemum parthenium syn.
Tanacetum parthenium
Chrysanthemum, feverfew
Height 45–60cm/18–24in

Spread 30cm/12in

This short-lived perennial is another plant
that has had its name changed and you
may also find it listed under *Tanacetum
parthenium*. The border varieties have
yellow or white flowers and some have
yellow leaves. The best are the double
forms, such as 'Plenum' and 'Snowball',
both white. Sow seed in late winter or
early spring at 10°C/50°F; take softwood
cuttings in spring.

Cineraria maritima
syn. *Senecio cineraria*

Height 20–30cm/8–12in

Spread 23–30cm/9–12in

The 'correct' name for this plant is now *Senecio cineraria* but you are far more likely to find it listed under its old name. It is the classic foliage bedding plant with silvery-white leaves that make an excellent foil to all colourful annuals. The best-known varieties are 'Silver Dust' and 'Cirrus'. Sow seed in spring at 20°C/68°F. If you can overwinter them you can take semi-ripe cuttings at the end of the summer.

Clarkia amoena
Satin flower

Height 75cm/30in

Spread 30cm/12in

Most attractive annuals with fluted flowers, sometimes with a marked centre. They can also be found listed as *Godetia amoena* and *G. grandiflora*. The flowers are usually pink, white or a deep lavender. The Satin Series is smaller. *C. unguiculata*, also sold as *C. elegans*, is larger with erect spikes of flowers, which in the Royal Bouquet Series look like small hollyhocks. Sow seed *in situ* in early spring, do not transplant. They make good dried flowers.

Consolida ajacis
Larkspur

Height 30–50cm/12–20in

Spread 15–25cm/6–10in

Attractive annuals grown for their erect spikes of flowers usually in soothing pastel colours of white, pale blue and pink, although some are deep violet. The smaller varieties are the ones most usually grown; Dwarf Hyacinth Series and Dwarf Rocket Series are both popular. They are strong plants and withstand wind well. The Giant Imperial Series is much larger, reaching 90cm/3ft, and should be planted at the back of a container or border. Hardy annual seed should be sown outside *in situ* in spring or the previous autumn. The plants are poisonous.

Convolvulus tricolor
Bindweed

Height 30–40cm/12–16in

Spread 23–30cm/9–12in

Common bindweed is one of the most pernicious garden weeds but its cultivated relations are charming plants and range from shrubs to annuals. *C. tricolor* is grown as a hardy annual. The series Flagship Mixed appears in a variety of colours: red, deep blue, light blue, white and pink. The trumpet-shaped flowers have strongly marked white and yellow centres. *C. sabatius* is a lovely blue hardy perennial normally grown in rock or scree gardens. It may need some protection in hard winters. Sow seed *in situ* in mid-spring. Take cuttings of perennials.

Coreopsis tinctoria
Tickseed

Height 30cm/12in

Spread 15cm/6in

The smaller tickseeds are varieties of *C. tinctoria*. The ones most usually grown are Dwarf Mixed or the variety 'Mahogany Midget'. The latter has bronze-red flowers with a yellow centre that are carried in profusion from midsummer until the autumn. *C. grandiflora* and its varieties are hardy perennials, sometimes grown as annuals, and usually have yellow flowers. 'Early Sunrise' and 'Mayfield Giant' are two good varieties. Sow seed *in situ* in spring.

Dianthus chinensis
Chinese pink, Indian pink

Height 15–25cm/6–10in

Spread 10–15cm/4–6in

Dianthus is a large genus with many different types of pinks and carnations that

Consolida ajacis

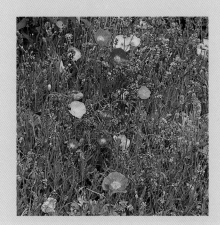
Eschscholzia californica

are grown both indoors and out. The common border pinks are those grown as half-hardy annuals where the seed is sown in spring at 16°C/60°F and the plants flower in late summer of that year. A number of series have been cultivated, and there are a number of named varieties. The Baby Doll and Carpet Series both have single flowers that range from red to white, but are mainly pink. The striking 'Raspberry Parfait' has pink flowers with deep red centres. Double Gaiety Series has double flowers in varying colours.

Erigeron karvinskianus
Midsummer daisy, Mexican daisy, fleabane
Height 15–30cm/6–12in
Spread to 90cm/3ft
This is an excellent plant to grow hanging down a wall, in a hanging basket or balcony container. Small daisy-like flowers emerge white in midsummer and then gradually turn through pink to red. If grown in a basket or window box it should be treated as a hardy annual; if grown

Fuchsia 'Tennessee Waltz'

down a wall it can be treated as a hardy perennial although it is very vigorous and may well need controlling. 'Profusion' is the variety most often grown. Sow seed in a cold frame in spring.

Eschscholzia californica
California poppy
Height 15–30cm/4–12in
Spread 15cm/6in
California poppies are one of the easiest of all plants to grow for the seed will take root anywhere, even in a gravel border. The plants self-seed vigorously and need to be controlled. They have single erect flowers on stalks in attractive colours, mainly yellow and orange, but some varieties are red, pink and white. The most spectacular is the Thai Silk Series that has semi-double flowers in a variety of colours. Sow seed *in situ* in spring.

Fuchsia
Fuchsia
Height (small varieties): 45–60cm/18–24in
Spread 30–60cm/12–24in
Fuchsias are mainly half-hardy shrubs, although there are some hardy varieties that will survive temperatures down to -5°C/23°F. They have pendent flowers, mostly in attractive pastel shades of pink, and many are bicoloured. They make excellent shrubs for hanging baskets and containers and can be brought indoors over winter where circumstances permit. Good varieties include: 'Margaret Brown', two-toned pink flowers; 'La Campanella', white and purple; and 'Swingtime', white double flowers with red outer petals.

Gazania
Height 20cm/8in
Spread 25cm/10in
Half-hardy perennials that are grown as half-hardy annuals. They are members of the daisy family and the flowers are daisy-like with rather broader petals. There are a number of series normally grown. The Chansonette Series has flowers in a mixture of colours: yellow, pink, red and orange. The Mini-star Series is smaller and has a wider range of colours. Sow seed in early spring at 18–20°C/64–68°F.

Heliotropium arborescens 'Marine'
Heliotrope, cherry pie
Height 30–45cm/12–18in
Spread 30–35cm/12–14in
Many varieties of *H. arborescens* make good sized shrubs, but the smaller varieties are usually grown as half-hardy annuals. 'Marine' is the most popular variety and has the characteristic smell of cherries that gives the plant its common name. 'Mini Marine' is a bit smaller and more compact. The flowers are violet blue and they make

Gazania

Lavatera trimestris 'Silver Cup'

a wide variety of colours: pink, cerise, red, white, some bicoloured, held above light green and bronze leaves, some of which can be variegated. They prefer to grow in partial shade and will even provide colour in complete shade, making them invaluable for gardeners with shady gardens. Many other series are available. Sow seed in spring at 16°C/60°F. You can take cuttings in summer to overwinter indoors.

Lavatera trimestris
Annual mallow

Height 60–90cm/2–3ft

Spread 30–45cm/12–18in

These are extremely attractive annuals, although some are a bit larger than most. They have that lovely mallow-shaped flower which is like a shallow trumpet. 'Pink Beauty' is white with pink veins on the petals and a darker centre, 'Silver Cup' is a deeper pink, and 'Mont Blanc' is almost pure white. Parade Series has pink, white and red flowers. Sow seed out of doors where the plants are to flower from mid-spring onwards.

excellent plants for containers in the summer. Seed can be sown in spring at 16°C/60°F but named varieties are best propagated by tip cuttings taken in summer, for they may not come true from seed.

Iberis umbellata
Common candytuft

Height 15–30cm/6–12in

Spread 20cm/8in

Another extremely popular hardy annual that should be sown out of doors where it is to flower in autumn or early spring. The two most popular series are Fairy Series, clusters of pale pink, lavender and white

flowers, and Flash Series, stronger colours of pink, purple or red. The flowers are made up of many small petals shaped like a shallow dome and completely cover the plant, giving rise to its common name, which is very descriptive.

Impatiens New Guinea Group
Busy Lizzie, balsam

Height 35cm/14in

Spread 30cm/12in

Almost the most popular summer bedding plant, busy Lizzies are half-hardy perennials although they are almost always grown as annuals. The New Guinea Group come in

Impatiens New Guinea Group

Limnanthes douglasii
Poached-egg plant

Height 15cm/6in

Spread 15cm/6in

An aptly named, low-growing annual, that has saucer-shaped flowers, white on the margin with deep yellow centres. It also has lovely bright green leaves. The flowers are attractive to bees and flower throughout the summer. It is easy to grow and seed should be sown *in situ* in spring or autumn for earlier flowering the next year. Autumn sowings need to be protected from frosts during the winter.

Linum grandiflorum
Flowering flax

Height 45–60cm/18–24in

Spread 15cm/6in

Flax flowers are supposed to be blue, and most perennial flaxes are, but the species plant of the annual flowering flax has rose-pink flowers. Of the named varieties 'Bright Eyes' is white, 'Caeruleum', blue, 'Magic Circles', red and white, and 'Rubrum', red. They are among the easiest of all hardy annuals to cultivate. Sow seed *in situ* outdoors in spring. Annual flax is best grown in blocks of colour so that it achieves its maximum effect.

Lobelia erinus
Trailing lobelia

Height 10–15cm/4–6in

Spread 15cm/6in

These are low-growing bushy perennials that are grown as annuals. They are the mainstay of hanging baskets throughout the world where the small flowers, generally blue with pale marked centres, hang down the sides. If grown in a rock garden they will fall over rocks and they look their best grown in a blue and white border with silver *Cineraria* (*Senecio*) and the white variety 'White Lady'. The Cascade Series has pink, red, blue and white flowers, Palace Series is mainly blue or white. There are border-edging and taller kinds available.

Matthiola incana
Gillyflower, sweet-scented stock

Height 20–45cm/8–18in

Spread 25–30cm/10–12in

Stocks are upright perennials or sub-shrubs but they are usually grown as half-hardy annuals. They are sometimes called 'ten-week stocks' for they achieve maturity quite quickly. They have upright spikes of flowers, usually white, red, pink and purple, and are very sweet-smelling. The Virginia stock, *Malcolmia maritima*, belongs to another genus. There are a number of series available. Brompton Series is grown as a biennial, Ten-Week Mixed has mostly double flowers and Sentinel Series is taller.

Mesembryanthemum criniflorum
Livingstone daisy

Height 8cm/3in

Spread 15cm/6in

Livingstone daisies are a popular half-hardy annual and flourish in dry conditions, but need sun to be at their best. The massed, typical daisy-like flowerheads are pink, white, cerise and yellow, with paler shades in between. They make good ground cover. Sow indoors in early spring at 16°C/60°F.

Mimulus × hybridus
Monkey flower, musk

Height 12–30cm/5–12in

Spread 30cm/12in

Tender perennials that are usually grown as annuals. There are a number of series: Calypso, Magic and Mystic are the ones usually grown. They have open trumpet-shaped flowers usually yellow or orange but creamy white, red and pink flowers are also found. They are often spotted in the centre. They prefer slightly damp soil. Sow seed indoors in spring at a temperature of 7°C/45°F or over.

Lobelia erinus

Matthiola incana

85

Nemesia strumosa
Nemesia

Height 20–30cm/8–12in

Spread 10–15cm/4–6in

Popular half-hardy annuals for the rock and scree garden, nemesias have charming, rather informal flowers that open into two halves and are often bicoloured. 'KLM' is blue and white, 'National Ensign' and 'Danish Flag' are both red and white. 'Blue Gem' is sapphire blue with white eyes and plants from the Carnival Series are smaller. Sow seed in spring at 15°C/59°F, or sow in autumn for early flowering the following year. Water the plants well when they come into flower and protect them from frost if they are to be overwintered.

Nicotiana × sanderae
Tobacco plant

Height 30–60cm/12–24in

Spread 20–45cm/8–18in

These are rather smaller than the traditional tobacco plant and the flowers are open during the day, not just in the evening. However they are not so fragrant.

'Lime Green' is a popular variety with green flowers. There are a number of series available, notably Domino, Havana and Roulette. They should be grown as half-hardy annuals. Sow seed in spring at 18°C/64°F. Plant out in the summer.

Petunia

Height 20–30cm/8–12in

Spread 30–90cm/12–36in.

Undoubtedly the most popular and widely grown of all summer bedding plants, petunias are half-hardy perennials that are almost always grown as annuals. They are divided into two groups: the Grandiflora varieties with large single flowers, and the Multiflora varieties that are bushier and produce a greater quantity of smaller flowers. The range of colours available is immense: single colours, double colours and many have variegated centre markings, either darker or in a second colour. The Supercascade Series is extremely popular for planting in hanging baskets, Carpet Mixed is an excellent bedding series and Delight Mixed has beautiful double

flowers. Sow seed outdoors in spring and deadhead flowering plants regularly through the summer to keep them flowering.

Pelargonium
Geranium

Height 12–60cm/5–24in

Spread 20–30cm/8–12in

A large genus of plants with six divisions. Those most commonly grown in borders are the Zonal geraniums and they have seven further subdivisions, depending on the flower shape. Trailing geraniums are excellent for window boxes on balconies, and also work well in hanging basket schemes. The flowers range from brilliant red, through all the varying shades of pink and purple, to white. Plants from the Horizon Series are compact and bushy – and good for containers – while those from the Orbit Series flower early. There are large numbers of named varieties. Geraniums can be raised from seed sown in spring at 16°C/60°F, but they are best propagated from softwood cuttings. These can be taken throughout the year.

Nicotiana x sanderae

Petunia

Sidalcea malviflora

Phlox drummondii
Annual phlox
Height 10–45cm/4–18in

Spread 20cm/8in

A pretty half-hardy annual that is grown for its attractive clusters of flowers that are slightly reminiscent of a small hydrangea. The flowers are generally white, purple, lavender, pink and red and the shades are very similar to many petunias. There are several series and they vary in size. Among the most popular are Twinkle Star Mixed with star-shaped petals. Fantasy Series is scented with clear colours and Palona Series is dwarf with bushy plants. Sow seed at 16°C/60°F early in spring, sow outdoors early in summer.

Salvia splendens
Scarlet sage
Height 30–40cm/12–16in

Spread 15–20cm/6–8in

Salvias are a large and varied genus but those grown as annual bedding plants have been developed from *S. splendens* that has such vivid red upright flowers in summer.

Tropaeolum majus

They are among the most popular bedding plants for the summer garden, and work well in a container. Several series have been developed. These include Sizzler, which can be found in eight colours, including salmon, deep pink, pale yellow, lavender, red and purple, and Phoenix Series. There are also many named varieties. Sow seed at 16°C/60°F in mid-spring.

Schizanthus pinnatus
Butterfly flower, poor man's orchid
Height 20–50cm/8–20in

Spread 20–30cm/8–12in

These are popular house plants when grown in a cool greenhouse but they can also be grown outside as hardy annuals, provided you have a warm sheltered border, and they can also be sown under glass over winter. They have attractive open tubular flowers held in clusters, which are generally white, yellow, pink, red and purple, and they have prominent yellow, or yellow-red central markings. 'Hit Parade' and 'Star Parade' are the ones most commonly grown. Sow seed at 16°C/60°F in spring or in late summer for plants to flower indoors during the winter.

Sidalcea malviflora
False mallow, prairie mallow
Height 30–90cm/12in–3ft

Spread 10–45cm/4–18in

Sidalceas are perennials that come from North America and flourish by the rivers and streams of the north and west. There are a number of varieties. They grow in almost any soil except when it is

waterlogged, and they prefer full sun. The best small varieties for a container garden are probably the compact 'Loveliness' with pale pink flowers, 'Puck', which has deeper pink flowers, or some of the special bedding mixtures. As might be imagined from their common name the flowers are open and saucer-shaped, and held upright on stalks above a rosette of basal leaves.

Tropaeolum majus
Nasturtium, Indian cress
Height 30cm/12in

Spread 45cm/18in

Popular climbing plants that are easy to grow in almost any soil and can be sown out of doors from late spring onwards. They do prefer a sunny position. There are a large number of varieties and these can be grown as bushy annuals or as semi-trailing plants in hanging baskets. They all have yellow and orange flowers in varying shades. The Whirlybird Series is popular as are the Double Gleam Mixed hybrids that have double flowers

Verbena × hybrida
Verbena
Height 30cm/12in

Spread 25cm/10in

Shrubby perennials that are grown as annual bedding plants. A number of series have been developed in a wide variety of colours from deep violet to blue, red, pink, peach and white. The flowers appear in clusters and each flowerhead is a bit like a very small primrose. Often they have a strongly marked centre. Some series are erect, others are trailing or spreading in habit, which makes them very suitable for hanging baskets and containers. Good series include Derby and Romance, both erect in habit. The Romance Series, and the varieties 'Peaches and Cream' and 'Imagination' are all spreading.

Viola × wittrockiana
Winter-flowering pansies

Height 20–30cm/8–12in

Spread 20–30cm/8–12in

The development of winter-flowering pansies has transformed gardens in the winter. They can be planted out in the autumn and will continue in flower for months on end. They are hardy perennials but should be treated as half-hardy annuals and fresh stock planted each year. Grow them in containers to provide individual bright spots in the garden. A huge number of series have been developed over the years, mostly multicoloured, or bicoloured, but single-coloured varieties are available. The colours run from deep violet and yellow, to purple, blue and white. Most varieties have the typical 'pansy' face with

Chionodoxa luciliae syn. gigantea

its strong central marking. The Fama, Regal and Ultima Series are all good winter-flowering plants; many other series flower in the summer.

Spring bulbs

Chionodoxa luciliae
Glory-of-the-snow

Height 15cm/6in

Spread 5cm/2in

Chionodoxa are less well known than many of the early spring bulbs but they are extremely attractive and deserve to be more widely grown. They have small, six-petalled, star-shaped flowers, in varying shades of blue, often with a pronounced white centre. Once established they self-seed readily. They prefer full sun. There are a number of varieties but the botanical names have become muddled. You will usually find them sold as *C. gigantea*, blue with white centre, *C. g.* 'Alba', white, *C. luciliae*, pale blue with white centre, *C. l.* 'Pink Cloud', pink, or *C. sardensis*, blue.

Fritillaria meleagris

Crocus chrysanthus
Spring-flowering crocus

Height 5cm/2in

Spread 5cm/2in

Crocuses flower both in the autumn and early spring, but it is the ones that flower early in the year that attract the most attention. The best known are varieties of *C. chrysanthus* and *C. tommasinius*. The majority are yellow, orange, purple to pale lilac, and white in colour. They are easy to grow given a certain amount of sun and well-drained soil. When the flowers open in spring they are a charming sight on a sunny day with the petals spread wide apart to catch the rays of the sun.

Cyclamen coum
Hardy cyclamen

Height 5cm/2in

Spread 10cm/4in

The hardy cyclamen that flower in spring are varieties of *C. coum*. *C. hederifolium* and its varieties look exactly the same but flower in autumn. Both species have attractive small white, pink, purple and red flowers held aloft on short stalks, a bit like upside-down small butterflies. They prefer soil that does not dry out but they need protection from excessive moisture and grow best in the shelter of trees or spreading shrubs. Mulch in the winter to protect the leaves from frost.

Narcissus
Daffodils, narcissus

Height 30–60cm/1–2ft

There are thousands of different daffodils available and a glance through the catalogue of any reputable bulb supplier gives some idea of the variety. There are 12 divisions. The best ones for the small container garden are varieties of *N. cyclamineus*, Division 6, which, in general gardening terms, would be called small narcissi. 'Peeping Tom' is pure yellow, 'Jack Snipe', white with yellow centre, 'Foundling', white with orange centre, and 'Jenny', white with white to pale yellow centre. Other good small varieties are those from Division 7, Jonquilla.

Erythronium dens-canis
Dog's tooth violet, trout lily
Height 10–15cm/4–6in

Spread 10cm/4in

The dog's tooth violet is another charming spring bulb that flowers slightly later than most spring bulbs. It needs moist, shady conditions and well-drained soil that does not dry out. It is grown for its attractive spotted foliage, which gives it the name of trout lily, as well the flowers that are held aloft on stalks with widely spaced, swept-back petals and long anthers. The best

Narcissus

known are 'Pagoda', yellow; 'Rose Queen', deep lilac-purple; 'Snowflake', white with pink markings. There are a number of other varieties available.

Fritillaria meleagris
Snake's head fritillary
Height 30cm/12in

Spread 5–7.5cm/2–3in

The snake's head fritillary is a popular bulb that is most often found naturalising in rough grassland. It is a good bulb to include in an alpine garden, for here its charms can be appreciated at close quarters. The bulbs need full sun to

flourish. *F. meleagris* is widely available with spotted purple flowers and there are white forms including *F. m. alba* and *F. m.* 'Aphrodite'. Other taller species that can be grown in the alpine garden include; *F. acmopetala*, green bell-shaped flowers flushed pink, and *F. camschatcensis*, black-purple flowers with yellow centres.

Hyacinthus orientalis
Hyacinth
Height 30cm/12in

Spread 7.5cm/3in

Hyacinths make excellent container-grown bulbs and are equally welcome planted in

Hyacinthus orientalis 'Pink Pearl'

autumn in prepared bulb fibre to flower
indoors in the early months of the year, or
grown in a container outside. The flowers
are held on long spikes and are extremely
fragrant. Plant hyacinths in groups of two
or three colours: white, lilac-blue and pink
are the most common and the most
effective. White hyacinths include,
'Carnegie' and 'L'Innocence'. 'Lady Derby'
and 'Pink Pearl' are pink, and 'Bluejacket'
and 'Delft Blue' are soft blue. Make sure to
stake the plants as they are liable to topple
over. Bulb suppliers sell special hyacinth
stakes for this purpose.

Iris reticulata and *I. unguicularis*
Early-flowering iris

Height 7.5–15cm and 3–6in/30cm/12in

Spread 2.5–5cm/1–2in and
30–45cm/12–18in

The bulbous irises known as reticulata are
the ones that flower early in the year along
with the rhizomatous *I. unguicularis* and its
varieties, which were formerly called *I.
stylosa*. They nearly all have lovely blue,
violet and yellow flowers with attractive

markings, although 'Natascha' is virtually
white. *I. danfordiae* has yellow flowers,
'Cantab', rich blue with a yellow stripe,
'Harmony', deep velvet blue. *I. unguicularis*
is pale blue to violet with a yellow band on
the fall; good varieties are 'Mary Barnard',
violet, and 'Walter Butt', a paler lavender.

Muscari armeniacum
Grape hyacinth

Height 20cm/8in

Spread 5cm/2in

Grape hyacinths are obliging plants for
they flower when many of the early spring
bulbs are over and they are easy to grow
and undemanding in their needs. The
flowers are usually differing shades of blue,
although violet-pink and white forms are
available. The most popular are varieties of
M. armeniacum, all of which have bright
blue flowers. They do colonise freely and
may require controlling when they are
grown in a restricted space.

Tulipa
Tulip

Height 15–65cm/5–26in

Spread 5–7.5cm/2–3in

There are so many different tulips of
varying colours and sizes that any container
gardener has to choose carefully according
to the colour scheme of the garden and the
space available. There are 14 divisions that
all flower at slightly different times, so if
you want a display all flowering together, it
is advisable to choose bulbs from the same
division. The colours range from yellow,
orange, pink and red, to deep purple,
almost black, back to white. There are a

number of striped and double coloured
varieties. Sturdy mid-season
tulips/Triumph, Group 3 include 'Douglas
Bader', pink, 'Golden Melody', yellow,
'Meissner Porzellan', white flushed pale
pink, and 'Prominence', deep red.

Summer- and autumn-flowering bulbs

Bulbs are not confined to the spring.
There are many lovely bulbs that flower in
the summer and autumn and a number of
these are worth considering for the
container garden.

Allium
Ornamental onions

Height 60–150cm/2–5ft

Spread 5–15cm/2–6in

Many ornamental onions flower in late
spring and early summer but there are
some that flower in late summer and into
autumn and the smaller varieties can add
much welcome colour to an alpine garden
in this period of the year. Among the best

Iris reticulata

Tulipa

is *A. sphaerocephalon* that reaches 60cm/2ft and has deep crimson flowerheads. *A. ostrowskianum* is an excellent rockery plant with heads of pink flowers in midsummer and *A. moly* is another small onion for the rockery with bright yellow flowers.

Alstromeria Ligtu hybrids
Peruvian lily
Height 50cm/20in

Spread 75cm/30in

Peruvian lilies are popular flowers for the summer container garden and should be grown in fairly deep containers, for the tubers should be planted at least 25cm/10in deep. They are best grown in individual containers for they can spread quite freely if they are given enough space. They have wide, flared flowers in varying shades of pastel colours, usually peach, orange, pink and creamy white. The colour varies considerably and they are a most welcome addition to a pale-coloured, delicate colour scheme in the summer. They prefer full sun.

Alstromeria Ligtu hybrids

Anemone coronaria
Windflower
Height 30–45cm/12–18in

Spread 15cm/6in

Anemones are tuberous perennials that should be left undisturbed when they have been planted. They like light sandy soil and full sun. *A. blanda* and its varieties flower early in spring and are common to many alpine garden planting schemes. Varieties of *A. coronaria* flower in late spring and early summer. These include the De Caen Group, single-flowered varieties, and the St Brigid Group, double-flowered varieties. The usual colours are red, blue, violet and white. The much taller Japanese anemones found in the herbaceous borders of the autumn are usually varieties of *A. hupehensis* or *A. × hybrida*.

Colchicum
Autumn crocus
Height 10–18cm/4–7in

Spread 7.5–10cm/3–4in

Colchicums are commonly known as autumn crocuses although in fact they have nothing to do with the spring bulbs. They are attractive bulbs with flowering stems that emerge before the leaves, giving them their other common name of Naked Ladies. The ones most usually grown are varieties of *C. agrippinum*, *C. autumnale* and *C. speciosum*. The most popular individual varieties are *C. s.* 'Album', large white globe-shaped flowers; *C.* 'The Giant', large purple-violet flowers; 'Violet Queen', pinkish-violet flowers; and 'Attlee', creamy white with large violet blotches on the ends of the petals.

Camassia
Common camassia, quamash
Height 75cm/30in

Spread 45cm/18in

Camassias are attractive summer-flowering bulbs with upright spires of flowers and tall mid-green leaves. The flowers are usually blue but vary in colour from white to purple and violet. The most commonly grown group is *C. leichtlinii* Caerulea Group that has purple-blue flowers. They prefer heavy moist soil and sun or partial shade. Divide the clumps when the plants are dormant and propagate by taking offsets from the parent bulb in the autumn.

Cardiocrinum giganteum
Giant lily
Height 1.5–2m/5–7ft

Spread 45cm/18in

The giant lily is a spectacular plant, even larger than the regal lily, and if grown in a container it will certainly require staking. It has creamy white funnel-shaped flowers that are fragrant and there are several flowers on each stalk. Plant the bulb just

Colchicum

Galtonia candicans

below the surface in moist rich soil. It prefers partial shade and will not flourish in direct sun. Take offsets from the main bulb after flowering.

Cyclamen hederifolium × neapolitanum
Baby cyclamen

Height 15cm/6in

Spread 20cm/8in

This is the autumn-flowering form of the hardy cyclamen. It is a tuberous perennial. The flowers appear from a corm before the leaves and are usually varying shades of pink; there are also white forms. They

flourish in dry shade and grow well beneath trees. The leaves, as the Latin name implies, are marked like ivy. The flowers self-seed freely in good conditions and eventually they form large colonies.

Galtonia candicans
Summer hyacinth

Height 90–120cm/3–4ft

Spread 10cm/4in

This is a large summer bulb that has beautiful spires of white flowers that hang down when the flowers finally emerge in late summer. The individual flowers are shaped rather like large snowdrops and

hang in much the same manner. They prefer to grow in good, fertile moist soil that does not dry out, in full sun. They are not totally hardy and containers of bulbs should be brought indoors in very hard winters. Two species are commonly grown: *G. candicans* and *G. viridiflora*. The flowers of the latter have a greenish tinge and they have a more upright habit.

Lilium
Lily

Height 90–150cm/3–5ft

Spread 25cm/10in

Lilies form a huge genus that has been divided into 9 main divisions and 11 sub-divisions. They make wonderful container plants; a large container filled with one variety can be a most effective focal point. All the large lilies need staking when they are planted. A number of them are exceptionally fragrant. Among the most popular are: *L. regale*, the regal lily, *L. candidum*, Madonna lily, *L.* 'Casa Blanca,' white, *L.* 'Citronella,' yellow, and *L. martagon*, the turkscap lily, purple.

Lilium 'Sunray'

Nerine bowdenii
Guernsey Lily

Height 35cm/15in

Spread 7.5cm/3in

Nerines used to be thought of as very tender and were only grown in greenhouses. However they are perfectly hardy in mild areas, as long as you can give them the shelter of a south- or southwest-facing wall. They have lovely pink trumpet-shaped flowers born in clumps in early autumn. The flowers last for quite a long time. The form *alba* has white, flushed pale pink flowers. 'Mark Fenwick' has deep pink flowers on dark stalks. They need to be left undisturbed after planting for they grow best when they are pot-bound.

Sparaxis
Harlequin flower

Height 10–25cm/4–10in

Spread 7.5cm/3in

These are cormous perennials that come from South Africa. There are 6 species but they are most commonly sold under the label Mixed Varieties. They are the most

attractive small summer plants, flowering from midsummer onward in varying shades of white through pink to red, each flower having a prominently marked central ring at the base of the petals with a yellow centre. A bowl full of them makes a wonderful display. They need full sun and are only suitable for growing in mild districts in temperate climates. They need protection in winter if grown out of doors.

Sprekelia formosissima
Aztec lily, Jacobean lily

Height 15–35cm/6–14in

Spread 15cm/6in

There is only one species of this lily but it is well worth growing as a house plant in temperate climates, although it flourishes out of doors when the temperature does not drop below 7°C/45°F. It has striking scarlet red flowers that give the impression that it is sticking out its tongue. When grown as a pot plant indoors, it needs full light and requires watering and feeding when in growth. It flowers in late spring or early summer. Keep dry when it is dormant.

Tigridia pavonia
Peacock flower, tiger flower

Height 40cm/16in

Spread 10cm/4in

Another unusual summer bulb that comes from Mexico and Guatemala where it grows in dry grassland, sand and occasionally among rocks. In temperate climates they should either be grown as pot plants and brought indoors in the winter, or in mild districts, planted out in a sunny border, lifted in the fall and brought indoors for the winter. They can also be grown permanently as container plants in a cool greenhouse or conservatory. They prefer well-drained, sandy, fertile soil. *T. pavonia* is a bulbous perennial with lance-shaped leaves. They are the most exotic looking plants – the flowers resemble orchids with their three large, white, pink, yellow and soft red outer petals, tiny inner petals, and contrasting central markings of vivid red and yellow spots. Sow seed at 13–18°C/55–64°F in spring. Separate offsets when dormant, avoiding plants affected by viruses.

Nerine bowdenii

Sparaxis Mixed Varieties

Tigridia pavonia

index

Abutilon 56
× suntense 56, 72
vitifolium 56
Abutilon megapotamicum 37
Acer palmatum 58
var. dissectum 64
aconite 49
'Adam' 12
'Adolphe Audusson' 43, 46
Aegeratum houstonianum 79
African lily 40
Agapanthus 40, 74
'Akashigata' 43, 46
'Aladdin Mixed' 13
'Alaska Mixed' 12
'Alberta Blue' 39, 67
'Alboplenum' 60
'Album' 41, 60, 91
Allium 90–1
moly 91
ostrowskinum 91
sphaerocephalon 91
Alstroemeria Ligtu Hybrids 54, 91
Alyssum spinosum 39
Amaranthus
caudatus 79
tricolor 79
'Amethyst' 78
'Andenken an Friedrich Hahn' 77
Anemone blanda 43
Anemone coronaria 91
'Anna Ford' 70
'Anne Marie' 48
antique wall pots 16
Antirrhinum majus 79
'Aphrodite' 89
Aponogeton distachyos 75
'Apple Blossom' 43, 46, 47, 61, 77
apples 53, 64
apricots 53
'April Tears' 35
aquilegia 23
Aquilegia vulgaris 75
arches 26–7
Argentea Group 78
Argyranthemum 26
'Arthur Turner' 64
Aster
novae-angliae 61
novi-belgii 40, 61, 75
'Attlee' 90
aubrieta 39, 79
Aubrieta × cultorum 79
'Aurea' 46, 66
'Aureovariegata' 67
'Aureus' 60
autumn 58–61
autumn crocus 60, 91
'Ave Maria' 43, 46
Aztec lily 93

'Baby Darling' 69
balloon flower 57
balsam 84
'Banana Milkshake' 13
'Barcos' 33
'Barry's Silver' 38, 46
bay 26, 27, 66
bay laurel 7
beauty bush 68
Begonia 33
semperflorens 79
tuberosa 79
Bellis perennis 79–80

Berberidopsis corallina 55
berries 58–60
'Bertie Ferris' 33
'Bianco' 70
Bidens ferulifolia 12
bindweed 82
'Bishop of Llandaff' 33, 35
'Blairii Number Two' 70
bleeding heart 75
blossom 52–3
'Blue Ball' 81
'Blue Bird' 52
blue cupidone 80–1
'Blue Danube' 79
'Blue Diadem' 81
'Blue Diamond' 52
'Blue Gem' 80, 86
'Blue Moon' 77
'Blue Pearl' 38
blue and white schemes 40–1
'Bluejacket' 90
Boston ivy 60
Bougainvillea glabra 55
'Boughton Dome' 57
'Boule de Neige' 56
Bourbon 70
'Bowles Dwarf' 47
'Bowles Hybrid' 57
box 22, 26, 67
Brachyscome iberidifolia 80
'Breakaway Red' 12
'Bressingham Blue' 40
'Bressingham White' 80
'The Bride' 51
'Bright Bikinis' 80
'Bright Eyes' 85
'Bright Gem' 35
'Bright Smile' 70
'Brilliant Star' 32
bulbs
autumn 60–1, 90–3
spring 50–1
summer 54, 90–3
'Burgundy Lace' 58
busy Lizzie 36, 84
'Butterfly' 58
butterfly flower 87
'Buxton's Variety' 41, 76
Buxus 26
sempervirens 22, 67

'Caeruleum' 85
Calamondin lemon 65
Calamondin orange 65
Calceolaria 80
Calendula officinalis 80
California poppy 83
'Californian Glory' 37, 56
Callistephus chinensis 80
Camassia 91
leichtlinii 91
camellia 42–3, 46, 47, 51
Camellia 47,
japonica 43, 46
× williamsii 43, 46, 65
Campanula carpatica 80
candituft 84
'Cantata' 35
Cape hyacinth 92
Cape pondweed 75
cardinal flower 77
Cardiocrinum giganteum 91–2
'Carnegie' 90
'Casa Blanca' 92
Catananche caerula 80–1
Cedrus deodara 66
Celebrity Bunting Series 13
Celebrity Mixed Series 13
Celebrity Pastel Mixed Series 13
celosia 32

Celosia
argentea 81
plumosa 81
Centaurea cyanus 32, 81
Ceratostigma willmottianum 61
Chaenomeles speciosa 37
Chamaecyparis lawsoniana 38, 46, 66
'Charmer' 43
cherry pie 83–4
'Chiffon Morn' 13
Chilean bellflower 74
Chilean potato vine 74
China aster 80
'China Pink' 51
Chinese pink 82–3
chionodoxa 23
Chionodoxa 39, 50, 51
gigantea 38
alba 38
luciliae 38, 51, 88
Christmas rose 48, 76
'Christopher Taylor' 35
Chrysanthemum parthenium 81
'Cilpinense' 52
Cineraria maritima 82
Cistus 40
× corbariensis 40
× cyprius 40
× Citrofortunella microcarpa 65
'Citronella' 92
citrus 65
Citrus limon 65
Clarkia
amoena 82
elegans 82
unguiculata 82
clematis 16, 28, 36, 52, 55
Clematis 36, 41, 48, 52, 55, 72, 73
alpina 36, 52, 72
armandii 52
balearica 48
cirrhosa 48
macropetala 36, 52
orientalis 36
tangutica 36, 60, 72–3
viticella 36
'Climbing Iceberg' 71
'Clive Greaves' 78
Colchicum 60, 90, 91
agrippinum 91
autumnale 60, 91
byzantinum 60
speciosum 60, 91
'Collyer's Gold' 46
Colour carpet 80
colour wheel 32, 42
columbine 75
'Compassion' 70–1
complementary colours 32
'Compressa' 46
'Comtesse de Bouchard' 55
'Concorde' 64
Confederate jasmine 56
Consolida ajacis 82
'Constance Spry' 71
Convolvulus
grandiflora 82
sabatius 82
tricolor 82
cool planting schemes 38–9
'Copenhagen' 71
Coreopsis
grandiflora 82
tinctoria 82
cornflower 32, 81
'Cornish Snow' 43, 46, 47
corydalis 23
crab apples 53, 58–9
Crambe cordifolia 40
cranesbill 41, 76

Crataegus 59
creeping bellflower 80
Crocosmia 33, 35
crocus 23, 49, 51, 88
Crocus
chrysanthus 38, 49, 88
tommasinianus 38, 88
vernus 38, 49
Cupid's dart 80–1
cyclamen 60, 88, 92
Cyclamen
coum 88
hederifolium 60, 88, 92
neapolitanum 61
Cytisus battandieri 37, 56
'Czar' 64

daffodil 34, 39, 50, 51
dahlia 35, 61
Dahlia 33, 35
daisy 79–80
damsons 64
'Danish Flag' 86
Daphne 47
cneorum 47
mezereum 47
odorata 47
day lily 35
'December Red' 47
'Delft Blue' 90
delphinium 40, 57
deodar cedar 66
'Depressa Aurea' 67
Deutzia 56
× elegantissima 56
'Devonia' 43, 46
Dianthus chinensis 82–3
Dicentra
formosa 75
alba 75
spectabilis 75
'Discovery' 53, 64
'Doc' 52
dog's tooth violet 50, 51, 89
doors 26–7
'Double Gleam' 12
'Douglas Bader' 90
'Douglasii' 46
'Doyenne du Commice' 64
drainage feet 15
'Dresden Doll' 70
Dutchman's trousers 75
'Dwarf Blue' 32
dwarf polyantha 70
Dwarf Russell Mixed 77

'E.A. Bowles' 49
'Early Sunrise' 82
'Early Transparent Gage' 64
Elaeagnus × ebbingei 47
'Elegantissima' 67
'Ena Harkness' 36
English rose 71
Eranthus hyemalis 49
Erica 38
carnea 38, 47
× darleyensis 38, 47
Erigeron karvinskianus 83
Erythronium 50, 51, 89
dens-canis 89
revolutum 51
Eschscholzia californica 83
'Etoile de Hollande' 36
Euphorbia
amygdaloides 75
characias 75
robbiae 75
'Eva' 12
'Eva Cullum' 78
evergreen shrubs 46–8

Exochorda × *macrantha* 51, 67

fair maids of February 48
'Fairy Damsel' 70
'Falcon White' 12
false cypress 66
false mallow 87
Fatsia japonica 67
features 24–5
'February Gold' 35
'Feelin' Blue' 66
'Fiesta' 64
firethorn 37, 47, 59, 74
flame creeper 56
flannel bush 56, 73
fleabane 83
'Flore Pleno' 35
'Florence Blue' 81
floribunda 71
floss flower 79
flowering flax 85
flowering maple 56, 72
focal points 22–3
forget-me-not 32
forsythia 51
Fothergilla major 58
'Foundling' 89
'Francis Joiner' 35
'Francis Rivis' 52
Fremontodendron 37, 56, 73
Fritillaria
    acmopetala 89
    camschatcensis 89
    meleagris 89
        alba 89
Fuchsia 83
fuchsia 83
'Fujiyama' 78
'Fusilier' 35

gages 53
Galanthus 48
Gallery Hybrids 77
Galtonia
    candicans 54, 92
    viridiflora 54, 92
'Garnet' 58
'Gateshead Festival' 35
Gaultheria
    mucronata 59
    shallon 59
'Gauntlettii' 43, 46
Gazania 83
'General Sikorski' 41
'General Vicomtesse de Vibraye' 68
'Gentle Touch' 70
Geranium 26, 36, 40, 41, 57, 86
    clarkei 41, 76
    farreri 76
    pratense 41
    psilostemon 76
    renardii 41
    sanguineum 41
    wallichianum 41, 76
'Giant' 91
giant lily 91–2
gillyflower 85
'Glacier' 12, 13, 73
Gladiolus 54
Glechoma hederacea 12
'Gloire de Marengo' 48
glory-of-the-snow 38, 39, 50, 88
Godetia
    amoena 82
    grandiflora 82
'Gold Cone' 46
'Gold Sovereign' 46
'Golden Chimes' 35
'Golden Fleece' 35
golden hop 60

'Golden Horizon' 66
'Golden Hornet' 59
'Golden Melody' 90
'Golden Showers' 36, 46, 71
'Goldflame' 52
'Goldquelle' 37
'Gorer's White' 56
Granny's bonnets 75
grape hyacinth 38, 39, 50, 51, 90
Greigii Group 34
'Guernsey Cream' 36
Guernsey lily 60, 93
'Gypsy Girl' 49

'H.F.Young' 41
half-barrels 14–15
× *Halimiocistus wintonensis* 68
hanging baskets 12–13, 17
'Hans Ricken' 35
harlequin flower 93
'Harmony' 39
hawthorn 59
Headbourne Hybrids 40, 74
Hebe 56–7, 68
    cupressoides 57
    pinguifolia 57
Hedera
    canariensis 48
    helix 12, 13, 48, 73
Helianthus × *multiflorus* 76
'Helios' 73
heliotrope 83–4
Heliotropium arborescens 83–4
Helleborus
    foetidus 48
    niger 48, 76
    orientalis 48, 76
Hemerocallis 33, 35
    fulva 35
'Henryi' 41, 55
herbs 28
'Hibernica' 46
'Hidcote' 26, 68
'Highgate Torch' 35
'Hit Parade' 87
holly 65
hollyhock 57
'Honeycomb' 12
'Horn of Plenty' 36
hosta 57, 77
Hosta 'Blue Moon' 77
hot planting schemes 34–7
house leek 16
Humulus lupulus 60
hyacinth 38, 50, 51, 89–90
Hyacinthus 38, 50, 51, 90
    orientalis 89–90
hybrid tea 72
hydrangea 21, 28, 56, 68
Hydrangea
    anomala 73
    macrophylla 68
    petiolaris 73

Iberis saxatilis 39
Iberis umbellata 84
Iceberg 26
Ilex aquifolium 65
Impatiens 36, 84
Indian cress 87
Indian Mallow 72
Indian pink 82–3
'Inspiration' 43, 46
iris 40, 48, 90
Iris
    danfordiae 90
    reticulata 90
    stylosa 90
    unguicularis 48, 90
ivy 12, 22, 48, 73

ivy-leaved cyclamen 92

'J.C. van Tol' 65
'Jack Snipe' 89
'Jackmanii Superba' 41, 55
Jacobean lily 54, 93
'James Mason' 41
Japanese aralia 67
Japanese maple 58, 64
japonica 37
jasmine 74
Jasminum
    nudiflorum 48
    officinale 74
'Jeanette Carter' 33
'Jeanne d'Arc' 49
'Jenny' 39, 75, 89
'Jewel' 80
'John Downie' 59
'John Huxtable' 41
'Johnson's Blue' 26, 41
Jonquilla 34, 89
'Joyce' 39
juniper 67
Juniperus
    communis 39, 46, 66, 67
    horizontalis 46
    × *media* 46

'Kashmir Blue' 41
'Kashmir Pink' 41
'Kashmir White' 41
'Katharina Zeimet' 70
'KLM' 86
knapweed 81
Kniphofia 37
Kolkwitzia amabilis 68
'Koster' 46
'Kristina' 75

'Lady Clare' 43, 46
'Lady de Sausmarez' 43
'Lady Derby' 90
'Lady Loch' 43, 46
'Lady Sunshine' 35
'Ladykiller' 38
lambs' ears 78–9
lambs' lugs 78–9
Lapageria rosea 74
larkspur 82
'Lascar Beauty' 43, 46
'Lassie' 75
'Lasurstern' 55
Laurus nobilis 26, 66
Lavandula angustifolia 26, 68
lavender 16, 29, 68
'Le Mahdi' 78
Lenten rose 48, 76
lettuce 53
Lilium 92
    candidum 92
    martagon 92
    regale 54, 92
        var. *album* 54
    speciosum var. *rubrum* 54
lily 54, 92
'Lime Green' 86
Limnanthes douglasii 85
'L'Innocence' 51, 90
Linum grandiflorum 85
'Little Flirt' 69
'Little Rainbow' 35
'Little Spire' 66
Livingstone daisy 85
lobelia 24, 25
Lobelia 12
    cardinalis 77
    erinus 77, 85
loosestrife 12

'Lord Derby' 64
'Lotus' 43, 46
love-lies-bleeding 79
Loveliness' 87
'Lucifer' 33, 35
Lulu Series 77
lungwort 53, 78
lupin 57, 77
Lupinus 77
'Lusty Lealand' 33
Lysimachia congestiflora 12

'Madame Julia Correvon' 36
Madonna lily 92
'Magic Circles' 85
'Mahogany Midget' 82
'Maigold' 36, 71
mallow 84
Malus domesticus 53, 64
'Marginata' 22
marguerite daisy 26
'Marie Ballard' 61, 74
'Marie Boisselot' 55
'Mariesii' 52, 57
marigold 80
'Marine' 83–4
'Mark Fenwick' 93
'Markham's Pink' 52
'Mary Barnard' 90
Matthiola incana 85
'Maurice Gibbs' 77
Mayfield Giant' 82
meadow saffron 60
'Meissner Porzellan' 90
Mesembryanthemum criniflorum 85
Mexican daisy 83
'Meyer' 65
Michaelmas daisy 40, 61, 75
midsummer daisy 83
Milady Mixed 80
milkweed 75
Mimulus × *hybridus* 85
miniature roses 69–70
'Minima' 46
'Moerheim' 52
monkey flower 85
'Mont Blanc' 84
'Mont Rose' 56
'Mother of Pearl' 59, 78
'Mrs Moon' 78
'Mrs Robb's bonnet' 75
Muscari 38, 39, 50
    armeniacum 51, 90
musk 85
Myosotis 32

naked ladies 60, 91
narcissus 35, 39, 88–9
Narcissus 50, 51, 88–9
    cyclamineus 35, 39, 89
nasturtium 12, 15, 87
'Natascha' 90
'National Ensign' 86
'Nelly Moser' 55
nemesia 86
Nemesia strumosa 86
Nerine bowdenii 60, 93
    alba 93
'New Dawn' 72
New England aster 61
Nicotiniana × *sanderae* 86
'Niobe' 36
'Nova' 35
Nymphaea 77

'Ohlendorffii' 67
Olea europa 27, 66
olive 27, 66
onion 90–1
'Opal' 64

'Orange Boy' 12
Ostrich Plume 80

'Pagei' 57
'Pagoda' 51, 89
pansy 13, 49, 88
Papaver 38
'Parkdirektor Riggers' 36
Parthenocissus
    quinquefolia 60
    tricuspidata 60
paths 28–9
patio rose 70
'Paul Lédé' 36
'Paul's Lemon Pillar' 36, 72
peaches 53
'Peaches and Cream' 88
peacock flower 54, 93
pearl bush 67
pears 53, 64
'Peeping Tom' 35, 39, 89
pelargonium 25, 28
Pelargonium 12, 86
'Pembury Blue' 46
penstemon 57, 77
Penstemon 26, 77
'Peregrine' 53
perennials
    autumn 61
    spring 53
    summer 57
periwinkle 13, 61
Pernettya 59
Peruvian lily 54, 91
petunia 24, 25, 26
Petunia 12, 13, 86
phlox 57, 78, 87
Phlox
    drummondii 87
    paniculata 78
Picea
    abies 67
    glauca 39, 67
    pungens 46
'Pickwick' 38, 49
pieri 51, 69
Pieris
    formosa 69
        var. *forrestii* 69
    japonica 51, 69
pincushion flower 57, 78
pineapple broom 37, 56
pink 57, 82–3
'Pink Beauty' 84
'Pink Pearl' 90
pink and red schemes 42–3
planning 20–1
plantain lily 77
Platycodon grandiflora 57
Plectranthus forsteri 12
'Pleniflorum' 60
'Plenum' 81
plums 53, 64
poached-egg plant 85
Poeticus 34
Polypodium vulgare 13
Pompon Mixed 80
poor man's orchid 87
poppy 37, 38
pot marigold 80
potatoes 7
pouch flower 80
'Pour toi' 70

prairie mallow 87
primary colours 32
primrose 16, 32, 78
Primula 16, 43, 49
    allionii 43
    vulgaris 32, 43, 78
'Prince of Orange' 78
Prince of Wales' feathers 81
'Prominence' 90
Prunus 52
    domestica 64
    persica 53
'Puck' 87
Pulmonaria 53
    saccharata 78
'Purpurea' 60, 75
Pyracantha 37, 47, 59, 74
Pyrus communis 64

quamash 91
'Queen Cox' 64

'R.L. Wheeler' 43, 46, 47
'Raffles' 67
raised beds 21
red cedar 67
'Red Joy' 35
'Red Marietta' 12
'Red Pygmy' 58
'Red Riding Hood' 35
'Red Rum' 35
red-hot poker 37
Reticulata 39
rhododendron 52
Rhododendron 52
    calostratum 52
    kiusianum 52
    sargentianum 52
rock rose 40
Rosa gallica 'Versicolor' 70
'Rose Queen' 89
'Rosealind' 56
rosemary 29
roses 23, 36, 42
    small 69–72
    types 26, 36, 41, 69, 70, 71, 72
'Rosie' 68
'Rosy O'Grady' 36, 52
'Rosy Pagoda' 52
'Rothesay Superb' 35
'Rowallene' 52
rowan 58
'Royal Picotee' 79
'Royal Ruby' 75
'Royalty' 43
'Rubella' 47
'Rubrum' 85
'Ruby' 36, 52
Rudbeckia laciniata 37
'Ruskin Diane' 35

Salvia splendens 37, 87
'Sapphire' 12
satin flower 82
Scabiosa
    caucasica 57, 78
    columbaria 78
scabious 57, 78
scarlet sage 87
Schizanthus pinnatus 87
Schizophragma hydrangeoides 56
scilla 50, 51
Scilla sibirica 39, 51

'Sealand Gem' 36
secondary colours 32
Sempervivum 16
Senecio cineraria 82
'Sensation Scarlet' 12
'Shakespeare' 35
shallon 59
'Shropshire Lad' 72
shrubs
    spring 51–2
    summer 55–7
    winter 46–8
Sidalcea malviflora 87
'Silver Cup' 84
'Silver Queen' 65
Single Early Group 34
skimmia 47
Skimmia japonica 47, 59
slipper flower 80
slipperwort 80
smaller containers 16–17
snake's head fritillary 89
snapdragons 79
'Snow Bunting' 49
Snow Lady' 52
'Snowball' 81
snowberry 59
snowdrop 48–9
'Snowflake' 12, 89
Solanum
    crispum 74
    jasminoides 74
Sparaxis 93
spiraea 69
Spiraea japonica 52, 69
Sprekelia formosissima 54, 93
spring 50–3
'Spring Festival' 43, 46
'Springwood Pink' 47
'Springwood White' 47
Stachys byzantina 78–9
'Stafford' 35
'Star Parade' 87
'Stardust' 66
'Stars 'n Stripes' 70
steps 28–9
stinking hellebore 48
'Stresa' 35
'Striatum' 41
'Stuart Boothman' 75
'Suffruticosa' 67
summer 54–7
summer jasmine 74
sunflower 76
'Sunset' 53
'Supercascade White' 13
Sutera cordata 12
'Swan Lake' 41
Swan River daisy 80
sweet bay 7, 66
'Sweet Dream' 70
sweet-scented stock 85
Symphoricarpos × doorenbosii 59

Tagetes 12
tall pots 15
Tanacetum parthenium 81
tassel flower 79
Taxus baccata 46
Thuja
    orientalis 67
    plicata 46
tickseed 82

tiger flower 93
Tigridia pavonia 54, 93
tobacco plant 86
tomatoes 7
'Tornado' 32
Trachelospermum jasminoides 56
trailing lobelia 85
'Trena' 39
Triandrus 34
Tropaeolum 15
    majus 12, 87
    speciosum 56
trout lily 89
tulip 34, 35, 38, 50, 51, 90
Tulipa 32, 34, 35, 51, 90
    clusiana var. *chrysantha* 35
    kaufmanniana 34, 51
    linefolia 35
    praestans 35
Turk's cap lily 92

Unwins Dwarf Group 33

'Vanguard' 49
verbena 87–8
Verbena × hybrida 87–8
'Veronica Tennant' 56
'Versicolor' 70
viburnum 52
Viburnum plicatum 52
'Vida Brown' 52
'Video Mixed' 12
'Ville de Lyon' 36
Vinca minor 13
'Vino' 36
viola 16
Viola × wittrockiana 13, 49, 88
'Violet Queen' 91
'Violetta' 72
Virginia creeper 60
Vitis
    coignetiae 60
    inconstans 60
    vinifera 60
'Vivelli' 47

'Wakehurst' 69
'Walter Butt' 90
'Wanda' 43
water hawthorn 75
water lily 77
'White Bedder' 26
'White Cockade' 41
'White Columbine' 52
'White Hedge' 59
'White Splendour' 43
white spruce 67
'White Swan' 43, 46, 52
'Williams Bon Chrétien' 64
windflower 91
window boxes 10–11
winter 46–9
winter jasmine 48
wood spurge 75

Yellow Doll' 69
'Yellow Gem' 35
yew 26

'Zéphirine Drouhin' 36

PICTURE CREDITS

Liz Eddison; Designer: David Brunn 15; Designer: Butler Landscapes, Chelsea 2000 20, 26; Designer: Alan Gardner 23; Designer: Lindsay Knight 21; Designer: Neil Holmes 54, 64bl, bc, 69bl, 73bl, tr, 74bl,br, 75bl, bc, 76br, 77bl, 78bl, 79bl, br, 80bl, 81bl, tr, 83bl, 86br, 88bc, 90bl, 91bl, 92tl, 93bl; Harry Smith Collection: 66, 29tr, 70bl, bc, 71bc, br, 72br, 82bl, 84tl, 85br, 93bc, br. Designer: Wynniatt-Husey Clarke, Hampton Court 2000; Illustrator: Ann Winterbottom back cover.